FAVORITE PICTURES

STAFF FOR THIS BOOK

EDITOR: Eric Levin
SENIOR EDITOR: Richard Burgheim
ART DIRECTOR: Anthony Wing Kosner
PHOTO EDITOR: Evie McKenna
CHIEF OF REPORTERS: Denise Lynch
ASSOCIATE ART DIRECTOR: Scott G. Weiss
SENIOR WRITER: Allison Adato
CONTRIBUTING WRITER: David Wallis
ASSISTANT PHOTO EDITORS: Ginger Propper, Jenny Rundgren
COPY EDITOR: Lance Kaplan
OPERATIONS: Barbara Scott

Special thanks to: Alan Anuskiewicz, Jane Bealer, Will Becker, Robert Britton, Betsy Castillo, Steven Cook, Sal Covarrubias, Orpha Davis, Nancy Eils, Brien Foy, Margery Frohlinger, Penny Hays, George W. Hill, Suzy Im, Rachael Littman, Eric Mischel, James Oberman, Stan Olson, Stephen Pabarue, Susan Radlauer, Helen Russell, John Silva, Céline Wojtala and the PEOPLE Technology Department

PREVIOUS PAGE: REGIS PHILBIN RAFAEL FUCHS 1999

IN THE MONEY: Chat host Regis Philbin began moonlighting from his daytime show in 1999 to ask the nearly rhetorical but rabidly irresistible question, "Who Wants to Be a Millionaire?"

COVER PICTURES, CLOCKWISE FROM TOP LEFT: TOM CRUISE (MARK LIDELL), BROOKE SHIELDS (ANDREW ECCLES), PRINCESS DIANA WITH PRINCES WILLIAM AND HARRY (PATRICK DEMARCHELIER), JOHN F. KENNEDY JR. (BETTY BURKE GALELLA/RON GALELLA LTD.), MICHELLE PFEIFFER WITH SASHA (BLAKE LITTLE), ROSIE O'DONNELL (JONATHAN EXLEY/ GAMMA LIAISON 1992).

8

46

73

99

contents

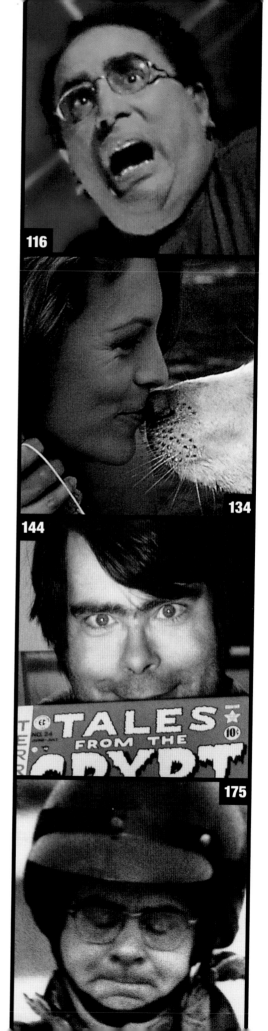

WHY THESE PICTURES

If the roughly 165,000 photos that have run in PEOPLE since its launch in 1974 were set end to end, we have no idea how far they would stretch; we just hope it wouldn't be a windy day. We do know that the bound volumes that hold all 26 years of weekly and special issues fill a wall of bookshelves in our library. We know because we have been through them and expended many packets of Post-its marking the pictures we found most compelling. Our goal was to reflect the range of PEOPLE photography—the glamour, the humor, the intimacy—as well as the weekly's evolution from black-and-white to color. We wanted to include a number of the most famous images ever taken for the magazine, yet present an abundance of gems unseen since they first ran in our pages. We hope you enjoy the book as much as we enjoyed putting it together. ERIC LEVIN

JACK NICHOLSON DOUGLAS KIRKLAND 1975

Hotshot Jack Nicholson and photographer Doug Kirkland proved to be a perfect match when PEOPLE paid a house call in Los Angeles on the combustible star of *One Flew Over the Cuckoo's Nest.*

Leading glittering—if, sadly, sometimes fleeting—lives on a plane above mere fame, these luminaries are the stuff of legends

FABUL

JOSEPH HELLER & DON SHAW
MICHAEL ABRAMSON 1982

Unsinkable

Stricken with Guillain-Barré syndrome, *Catch-22* author Joseph Heller spent several months in bed as the disease ran its paralyzing course. At home, he worked to regain his strength through physical therapy, like this pool exercise. He recovered, wed one of his nurses and lived another vibrant 17 years.

LANCE ARMSTRONG
JEAN-PAUL PELISSIER 1999

Joie de Vivre

Against all odds, Texan Lance Armstrong, 27, won the Tour de France, cycling's greatest prize, just three years after surgery and chemo for testicular cancer that had spread to his brain, lungs and abdomen. Armstrong might argue that an even bigger triumph of the year was the birth of his son, Luke, three months after the race.

An Affair to Remember

When asked the secret of a successful marriage, George Burns would reply, "The answer's easy: Marry Gracie." When his ditzy costar Gracie Allen died in 1964, Burns built a mausoleum for her at L.A.'s Forest Lawn cemetery and paid a monthly visit. "You cry and you cry. And finally there are no more tears, and you go back to work," said Burns, who won an Oscar a decade later at 79 for *The Sunshine Boys*. In his act Burns, who performed well into his 90s and died at 100, routinely joked about mortality, explaining, "I know Gracie's up there. And if they've got vaudeville, we can be headliners."

GEORGE BURNS
HARRY BENSON
1988

A Brother's Blues

Sidekick status always fit Dan Aykroyd as comfortably as a black gabardine suit, fedora and shades. But when his comedy partner John Belushi died at 33 of a drug overdose, Aykroyd led his pal's funeral procession—and rolled on. He stretched himself as an actor, starring in *Ghostbusters* and picking up an Oscar nomination for *Driving Miss Daisy*. And he honored Belushi by producing, writing and directing a sequel, *Blues Brothers 2000*. Said Aykroyd: "I miss him all the time."

DAN AYKROYD
DOUG BRUCE
1982

BACK COVER, TOP: GLENN CLOSE THOMAS VICTOR 1982

Glenn Close didn't do handsprings about being cast as Robin Williams' mom, but *The World According to Garp* catapulted her to stardom.

BACK COVER, BOTTOM: MIA FARROW JONATHAN EXLEY 1997

At the time of Mia Farrow's memoir, seven of her 14 children still lived at her Connecticut home, including Isaiah, 5, and Kaeli-Shea, 3.

PRINCESS DIANA & JOHN TRAVOLTA
PETE SOUZA 1985

A Sad Turn At a fête in the Reagan White House, Princess Diana twirled with John Travolta, creating a defining photograph for the ages. But her fairy-tale marriage flamed out like a flashbulb. She became a single mum of two heirs to the British throne, and had only a few years to find a new life when she died in a 1997 car crash while fleeing the paparazzi. She was 36.

OSITY

RON HOWARD, TOM HANKS & DARYL HANNAH
MARK SENNET 1984

Star Fish

Ron Howard had only recently convinced Hollywood that the artist formerly known as Opie could direct. For *Splash,* his second feature, Howard gave a break to newcomers Tom Hanks and Daryl Hannah as an interspecies couple. Hannah would shed the fins for more significant roles in *Wall Street* and *Steel Magnolias,* while Howard and Hanks enjoyed stratospheric careers (the latter winning two Best Actor Oscars) that paired them up again in 1995's *Apollo 13.*

TORI SPELLING
HARRY BENSON 1992

Fast Lane "I never wanted to be driven around in a limo," insisted Tori Spelling, as she took the wheel of her BMW and her accelerating career. "I've finally stopped being Aaron Spelling's daughter," declared the star of his *Beverly Hills, 90210*. "The greatest thing is when we go out together and the photographers say, 'Uh, Tori, can we get some of you alone?'"

TOM CRUISE
MARK LIDELL 1999

Frisky Business

Growing up in New Jersey, Tom Cruise mowed lawns for $5 a pop. Now he commands more than $20 million per film, $70 million for *Mission Impossible* alone. (Of course, his 20-plus movies have grossed more than $3 billion worldwide.) He also has a working wife in Nicole Kidman. But the high school dropout can't forget his scrambling start. "I push myself," he says. "I've never walked through anything."

GEORGE CLOONEY & KELLY PRESTON
NEAL PRESTON 1989

Who's on Top?

Kelly Preston and George Clooney chose different paths after their romance fizzled. She married John Travolta, became a mom and acted occasionally; Hollywood's most eligible bachelor chased his star, headlining TV's *ER* and films like *Three Kings.* "George," says pal Tom Hinkley, "believes you either have a career or you have love."

Yakity-Yak

Having scrabbled up from nightclubs to her own talk show, Joan Rivers was a survivor in the cutthroat comedy world. But in 1987 she felt tragedy might swallow her up: Her beloved husband, Edgar Rosenberg, killed himself after suffering a heart attack. "He was my rock," she wrote in a 1991 memoir. "Nothing would be the same." And

JOAN RIVERS
HARRY BENSON
1991

it wasn't. But she came back from depression, returning to work as the catty fashion commentator for E!, a job she often shared with daughter Melissa. Ever fashionable herself, she and her Yorkie Spike kept stylists at her beck and call, adding to the rubbernecking on New York's Fifth Avenue.

Naked Truth

"Bo is a movie star," insisted one producer. "Maybe not an actress, but a movie star." As surely as Bo Derek could count on top billing in any of husband John's films, so too could she depend on horrendous reviews. Starring in *Tarzan, the Ape Man* and *Bolero,* she had little to cover her body or her inexperience. In 1998, over John's objections and after his death, the movie star tried a TV series which NBC killed after two airings.

BO DEREK
JOHN DEREK
1984

Double Take

"Let them think it's Tahiti, even if it's Burbank," declared Angie Dickinson (at her home in Beverly Hills). She was disappointed when her *Dressed to Kill* director Brian DePalma tattled about using a 23-year-old body double for the then-48-year-old star in shower scenes: "Why destroy the illusion?" In her 60s she became an Alzheimer's fund-raiser but remained ever mindful of her looks. "It's a fight," she says, "all the way."

ANGIE DICKINSON
MARK SENNET
1980

MARK SENNET/REFLEX

FRED & ROBYN ASTAIRE
HARRY BENSON 1981

Young at Heart

If Fred Astaire still had a spring in his step at 81, it was partly due to his wife, Robyn Smith, 43 years his junior. She gave up a winning career as a jockey to wed the virtually retired star. "He still likes to make a buck," she teased, but she was content to ride nothing wilder than her bike. After some 40 films, Astaire just hung at their L.A. canyon home, playing backgammon and watching soaps. He died six years later, in his wife's arms.

Heartbreaker

The year PEOPLE named him the Sexiest Man Alive, John F. Kennedy Jr. was a law student trying to forge an identity beyond his famous name and good looks. When he worked for the New York D.A., many guessed he might run for office. But then he left the law to found

JOHN F. KENNEDY JR.
BETTY BURKE
GALELLA 1979

George, a political pop-culture magazine. By 1999, seemingly comfortable in his role as editor and quiet philanthropist, Kennedy, 38, and wife Caroline Bessette, 33, died when his plane plunged into the sea.

Fever Pitch

After four years in TV high school, it was time for Vinnie Barbarino to graduate. John Travolta left *Welcome Back, Kotter* to make an R-rated film (bummer for kid fans) about a Brooklyn disco king. *Saturday Night Fever* won him, at 23, an Oscar nomination. After 1978's *Grease,* his star power seemed permanent. But then came duds like *Perfect.* He wed Kelly Preston, had two kids and rocketed back into the firmament with 1994's *Pulp Fiction. Battleship Earth,* in 2000, was based on a sci-fi novel by Travolta's spiritual guru, Scientology founder L. Ron Hubbard.

JOHN TRAVOLTA
KEN REGAN
1977

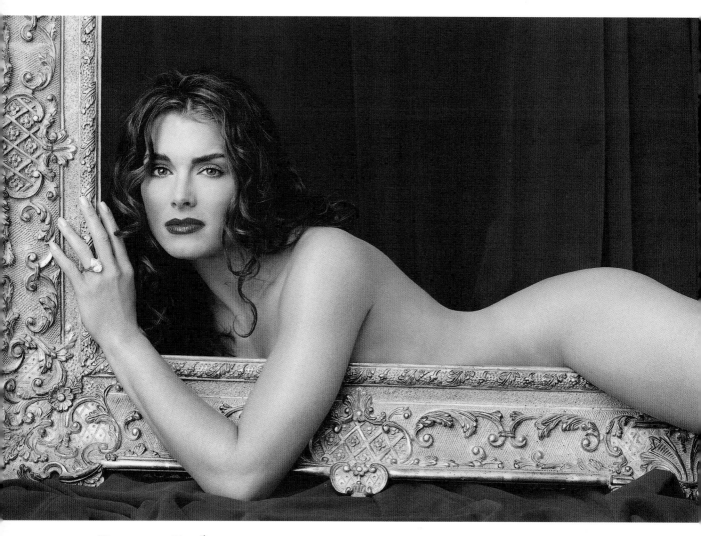

Pretty, Baby

A teen model notable for having nothing come between her and her Calvins, Brooke Shields had made her film debut, including a brief nude scene at 12, as a prostitute in Louis Malle's *Pretty Baby* (1978). Her subsequent choices (*The Blue Lagoon, Sahara*), guided with a heavy hand by mother and manager Teri, proved disastrous. Shields escaped the onslaught to attend Princeton and by the mid-1990s got back on track by showing she was pretty funny too. No longer managed by Mom, she starred in the NBC sitcom *Suddenly Susan* and posed provocatively here at 33 for PEOPLE's 25th anniversary.

BROOKE SHIELDS
ANDREW ECCLES
1999

LITTLE RICHARD
DANA FINEMAN 1984

Lordy!

At 51, Little Richard Penniman was on a second hiatus from rock 'n' roll and its excesses, having dedicated himself to Christianity. He stayed off drugs but later returned to touring. In 2000, his saga was turned into a TV biopic. Though he was one of the film's producers, he had some qualms about the depiction. Among them: "They didn't use near enough makeup."

A-LIST PREMIERE
ALEX BERLINER 2000

Love Your Hair!

Brad, Benjamin . . . Benjamin, Brad. Julia, Jennifer. . . Jennifer, Julia. Were introductions really necessary? At the L.A. premiere of Roberts' smash *Erin Brockovich*, she and Pitt, her costar in the upcoming *The Mexican*, offered up their significant others, Bratt and Aniston, respectively.

CHARLIE'S ANGELS
JULIAN WASSER
1976

Bimbo Eruption

Though tame compared to today's prurient prime-time lineup, *Charlie's Angels* unleashed an outcry when it jiggled to the top of the Nielsens. "Massage parlor TV," railed one of the show's critics, who ran the gamut from fundamentalists to women's libbers. The tumult only attracted more viewers, as Aaron Spelling's series about three underclad undercover officers (from left: Jaclyn Smith, Farrah Fawcett and Kate Jackson) and their chaperone Bosley (David Doyle) ushered in the Age of the Fox before that became the name of a network. "Up to that point, detective shows almost all had men as the leads," observed Smith. "All of a sudden three girls came along. That's feminist, not sexist. In our own small way, maybe we helped open the door a little bit for women."

KEN REGAN/CAMERA 5

Toned Down
When she burst onto the scene in the 1980s, Madonna was totally tuned, all lace-and-skin and swinging crucifixes. But as the century flickered out, she was more likely to be found at Gymboree than the gym. In 1996, she and her then boyfriend, trainer Carlos Leon, welcomed daughter Lourdes. By 2000 she had a new man, British director Guy Ritchie, and was pregnant again. Why? Her child had become a prima-madonna, "incredibly spoiled," worried Mom. "She needs a little competition."

MADONNA
KEN REGAN
1985

Well, Hello Yourself
By the mid-1970s Dolly Parton could look in the mirror and see, as she put it, "a trashy-looking blond country singer." Or she could look beneath the self-invented glitz and glimpse traces of the Smoky Mountain girl who grew up in a dirt-floor cabin, playing a mandolin she'd made from an abandoned piano wire. Even as a country superstar, she never roamed far from her Pigeon Forge, Tennessee, home. "My roots run deep," she said. "And this place keeps me sane in a crazy world."

DOLLY PARTON
HARRY BENSON
1976

The Me-llionaire

Like the mythological Narcissus, Donald Trump seemed simply besotted, preening in front of a floor-to-ceiling mirror. Trump palpably yearned for attention, plastering his name on gilded towers, casinos, an airline (that failed) and four vanity tomes. Even his ugly divorce from Ivana—"Don't get mad, get everything" was her famous war cry—proved an opportunity to elevate his skyscraper ego; he was reportedly gleeful as the sordid details of his affair with model Marla

DONALD TRUMP
HARRY BENSON
1990

Maples (whom he later wed and dumped) played out for months in New York City's tabloids. As a topper in 2000, Trump publicly flirted with running for President, no doubt blinded by visions of global summits and blaring fanfares of Hail to the Donald.

Dervish Diva
No wonder Mariah Carey needed to hang out on her couch—her career kept spinning at 78 rpm. The onetime waitress struck Grammy gold at 21, netting five nominations for her debut album in 1991. Since then, Carey, known for her soulful ballads (and provocative wardrobe), has sold more than 80 million records, spending more time atop Billboard's singles chart than any act except Elvis and the Beatles. Along the way she jettisoned her controlling husband, Sony Music chief Tommy Mottola. "[Mariah is] growing," noted her friend Debbie Allen. "She's come out of her cocoon, and she's spreading those wings."

MARIAH CAREY
JOHN
LOENGARD
1991

ANDY WARHOL & CO. AT STUDIO 54 ROBIN PLATZER 1977

Night Fever As the Me Decade convulsed to a decadent climax, the glitterati air-kissed, discoed and drugged until dawn at New York City's Studio 54. Here (from left) Halston, Bianca Jagger, Jack Haley, his then-wife Liza Minnelli and Andy Warhol celebrate New Year's Eve. In a typical entry from his posthumously published diary, Warhol, the club Boswell, described a writer watching "Bianca take poppers and [telling fashion guru] Diana Vreeland, 'It becomes more like pagan Rome every day.' And she said, 'I should hope so—isn't that what we're after?'"

Fresh Face

Unhappy with the nothing parts he was getting in nothing movies like *Mall Rats,* Ben Affleck teamed with pal Matt Damon to bang out a script with a leading role for each of them. *Good Will Hunting* made them stars and won them a writing Oscar. Then life got even better for the college dropout from a working-class Boston neighborhood. Without having to type another word, he got leads in big-budget spectacles like *Armageddon.* He also landed on the arm of Hollywood royal Gwyneth Paltrow. "Ben," understates his producer pal Chris Moore, "is having a good time."

BEN AFFLECK
ANDREW HALL
1998

Lethal Weapon

Killer blue eyes helped a recent Australian acting-school grad get his first role in *Mad Max,* even though he had been in a bar fight the night before the audition. His face, he said, looked "like a busted grapefruit." Mel Gibson's breakthrough in his native U.S. was 1983's *Year of Living Dangerously.* Since then, Gibson has amassed box office receipts of $1 billion and two Oscars for his 1995 directing debut, *Braveheart.* Offscreen the movie idol is a devout

MEL GIBSON
KEN REGAN
1983

Catholic and family man, with seven kids and a wife, Robyn, of 19 years.

Net Gain

Dude, who could have, like, guessed it? Keanu Reeves, the vernacularly challenged star of *Bill and Ted's Excellent Adventure,* grew up to, among other things, star in *Much Ado About Nothing* with Kenneth Branagh, and to carry the strangest, hippest sci-fi flick at millennium's end. Five years earlier the Canadian actor saw his action-hero potential take off with *Speed.* But about acting, he said, "I don't know anything, man." He did know enough to take the 1999

KEANU REEVES
JEFFREY
NEWBURY
1995

computer-hacker role in the breakthrough hit *The Matrix.* Awesome.

Serene Highness

Pictured in the palace just months before her death in a car crash following a stroke, Princess Grace, 52, ruled two constituencies: her adopted Monaco and movie fans everywhere. The always elegant daughter of a Philadelphia bricklayer turned millionaire contractor had abdicated Hollywood to marry her prince. Summed up director Alfred Hitchcock: "They all said at first she was too cold, but to me she was a snow-covered volcano."

Deliverance
Loni Anderson no longer looms over Burt Reynolds' shoulder; in 1994 the couple's clamorous, high-octane marriage ran out of gas. Reynolds' movie career also stalled, as he took roles in a string of flops like *Striptease,* which he said consigned him to "the nostalgia section of Blockbuster" and left him in bankruptcy. But by 1997, Reynolds had rebounded in *Boogie Nights,* portraying a sleazy yet sensitive pornographer in a role that earned him his first Oscar nomination.

BURT REYNOLDS
HARRY BENSON
1981

MICHAEL J. FOX
TONY COSTA 1987

Turning Tables

Even after his triumph in TV's *Family Ties* and the *Back to the Future* films, Michael J. Fox never trusted his success, once explaining, "I'm afraid that if I slow down, somebody is going to come up and say it was all a mistake." Then in the 1990s, he was struck by Parkinson's disease. At first, Fox continued to carry NBC's popular *Spin City*, though without medication he sometimes could barely pick up a TV remote. Finally, in 1999, he announced he would leave the series to join the public fight against Parkinson's and devote more time to wife Tracy Pollan and their three children. "My family," he declared, "is the reason I live."

Home Bodies

Away from the circuit or the set or those preying paparazzi, the famous chilled and let loose on their own turf

Happy Landings

Fun was often the order of business when best pals Penny Marshall and Carrie Fisher got together (here, the former Princess Leia takes flight on Marshall's bed). Libras both, the two celebrated their birthdays in joint bashes for two decades—missing only three, one when Fisher wedded Paul Simon. Marshall could relate to Fisher's problem of being known for one iconic role, having spent seven years as TV's Laverne. And both rebounded to shatter Hollywood's glass ceiling, Marshall as a director (*Big, Awakenings*), Fisher as a script doctor and novelist who penned *Postcards from the Edge.*

PENNY MARSHALL & CARRIE FISHER
TONY COSTA
1991

TONY COSTA/CORBIS OUTLINE

Re-Booted

In the 1970s, Elton John's music and outrageous getups made him a star and wealthy beyond his own imagination. (His eyeglass collection alone cost $40,000.) The press celebrated his splendor, but nosed around for evidence of a lady friend. By the 1990s he found he could talk comfortably about being gay, and ventured away from rock to score Disney's *Lion King* and a new version of *Aida*. John, who now favors Versace suits, says the opera update "is one of the things I'm most proud of in my career."

ELTON JOHN
TERRY O'NEILL
1975

Hideaway

Recording hits like "Anticipation" and "You're So Vain" came easily to Carly Simon. But performing them was problematic. A 1981 anxiety attack kept her offstage for nearly a decade. Yet even after her concert comeback, Simon preferred to pass a quiet evening in her Martha's Vineyard home with Sally and Ben, her children with ex-husband James Taylor. "Bedtime, when I read to the kids," she said, "is still sacred."

CARLY SIMON
JOE McNALLY
1987

TERRY O'NEILL/CORBIS SYGMA

Rancho Mirage

Welcome to Neverland, the California fun-and-game park that Michael Jackson calls home. The mountainous, 2,700-acre spread boasts a Ferris wheel, carousel, petting zoo and two-story arcade to entertain Jackson's youthful entourage but has been a whammy-land for wedlock (including for chum Elizabeth Taylor, who married Larry Fortensky there). It was Jackson's over-attention to young visitors that reportedly doomed his 20-month marriage to Lisa Marie Presley; he, in turn, felt frustrated at her refusal to have a family. Enter Debbie Rowe—a Harley-riding assistant to the singer's dermatologist—who wed Jackson the year of his split. Rowe bore him a son (Michael Jr., nicknamed Prince) and a daughter (Paris), then filed for divorce after three years of minimal togetherness.

MICHAEL JACKSON
HARRY BENSON
1993

Cooking with Pam

Discovered at a football game when a TV camera's gaze settled on her fair splendor, Pamela Anderson parlayed that accidental exposure into a TV career. On *Baywatch* the British Columbia native became a California icon, saving wayward surfers weekly. But her romantic life was far less buoyant. With rocker Tommy Lee she had two sons and an on-and-off marriage. Now single, she produces and stars in *V.I.P.,* a campy action show. "I love the dumb blonde image," she professed. "Then I have nothing to live up to. I can only surprise people."

PAMELA ANDERSON
GWENDOLEN CATES
1993

Toast of Nashville

Tammy Wynette and George Jones recorded country music's most beloved duets. Too bad they didn't get along as harmoniously outside the studio. Five years after their 1975 divorce (Wynette was by then married to manager George Richey), the pair reunited for a new song. Jones, recently on the wagon, toasted their success with grape soda. But hard times lay before them: Both would file for bankruptcy. They met again in 1995 to sing one for the road. Wynette died three years later at 56.

TAMMY WYNETTE & GEORGE JONES
SLICK LAWSON
1980

Fiddling Around
Alison Krauss was just 12 when musician John Pennell heard her stunning voice. Soon he learned that the youngster from Champaign, Illinois, was also a promising fiddler. "She never practiced till John came along," recalled her father, a onetime opera singer. A decade later, Krauss was a Grammy-winning bluegrass artist, and Pennell, 44, who wrote some of her best tunes, remained a friend and frequent visitor for jam sessions in the family kitchen.

ALISON KRAUSS & JOHN PENNELL
JAMES SCHNEPF
1994

A Doll's House

Her younger sister Maureen deploys a time-tested tactic to irritate Rosie O'Donnell: She surreptitiously shifts around some of the thousands of toys displayed on custom-built shelves in the talk show host's New York City apartment. "If you take one and put it in the wrong spot, she can pick it out in a second," says Maureen (a New Jersey homemaker). Rosie's collection, which her toddler Parker refers to as "Mama toys," includes pop culture artifacts from her childhood—such as an original 1960 *Chatty Cathy* doll, *I Dream of Jeannie* miniatures and *Star Trek* figurines—as well as knickknacks like the 2,500-odd McDonald's Happy Meal toys she picked up while on the stand-up circuit in the mid-1980s. "In bed at night, I think about where they should go," admits Rosie. "I'm so anal-retentive about them. I'm like *Rain Man.*"

ROSIE O'DONNELL
NEAL PRESTON
1997

Mourning Room

Shortly after a seven-day bedside vigil in which her 19-year-old son emerged from a coma following a near-fatal car accident, talk show host Sally Jessy Raphaël lost her oldest daughter. Allison Vladimir, 33, had died at an historic Pennsylvania inn owned by her mother and stepfather after taking a lethal combination of prescription and over-the-counter drugs to alleviate her chronic back pain. Vladimir was an established, Paris-trained chef, and Raphaël said she'd never be able to celebrate holidays again ("We go away to where they don't have Thanksgiving"). Raphaël sought solace in her departed daughter's doll-filled bedroom in the family home at Montrose, New York. "I have times when I'm more at peace," she said. "But there will always be this pain inside."

SALLY JESSY RAPHAËL
CHRISTOPHER LITTLE
1992

NEAL PRESTON/OUTLINE

Prime Time After years of going to bed at 5:30 p.m. in order to rise at 1 a.m. to prepare for her *CBS Morning News,* Diane Sawyer rejoiced at her liberation to *60 Minutes.* She would stay on the late shift for *Prime Time Live* after she jumped to ABC. But when ratings for that network's morning show dipped in 1999, Sawyer was again setting a dawn alarm to try to rescue *Good Morning America.*

Show Me the . . .

"It's provocative," said Jack Nicholson of the platter of shredded money he displayed on his coffee table. "It creates more interest than any other art in the room." That included a Magritte and a Rodin, purchased by the star, who went on to collect three Oscars. Then 43, Nicholson shared his L.A. hilltop home with Anjelica Huston, 29. In 1989, the pair separated after 17 years and infidelities on both sides, she with Ryan O'Neal, he with Rebecca Broussard, later the mother of two of his children. (First daughter Jennifer was the product of a marriage in the 1960s.) As the century turned, Nicholson, 62, had a new 29-year-old partner, actress Lara Flynn Boyle.

JACK NICHOLSON
TONY COSTA
1980

Rope-a-Hope

Parkinson's disease prevents the once amazingly graceful Muhammad Ali from floating like a butterfly, but he can still mug like a pro. Ali (watching his favorite boxer on tape at home in Berrien Springs, Michigan) relies on his faith and charity work to beat the blues. He travels about 275 days a year, making the rounds at fund-raisers and hospital wards, where he mixes it up with patients. "One day you wake up and its Judgment Day," says Ali. "So you do good deeds. I love sick people. I don't worry about disease. Allah will protect me. He always does."

MUHAMMAD ALI
HOWARD BINGHAM
1997

Oh, Grow Up

On camera and off, Johnny Depp often behaved like an overgrown kid. The star of *Cry-Baby* (here in his Hollywood home) attacked a photographer in London, trashed a Manhattan hotel room in a drunken rage and nearly flambéed his boyish face when he spit gasoline at an open flame. But Depp seemed to mature after having a daughter with actress-singer Vanessa Paradis. "I feel like there was a fog in front of my eyes for 36 years," he said. "The second she was born, that fog just lifted."

JOHNNY DEPP
LANCE STAEDLER
1994

Hit Single

Adored overseas, Julio Iglesias bemoaned his image in the U.S.: "They know me for selling too many records and making love to too many women." Well, yeah. After his 1978 divorce from Madrid journalist Isabel Preysler, who raised the couple's three children, Iglesias did get around. "If you commit your brains and heart to another, you can no longer fight," said the singer (at home in Miami). "I need to fight." In 1997

JULIO IGLESIAS
NEAL PRESTON
1988

he and Miranda Rijnsburger, a Dutch model, had the first of two kids. Yet unremarried, Iglesias may still battle for the title of Most Eligible Continental Crooner. Though now his son Enrique, 24, is also on the charts.

Bellissima!

"The girl makes you think all the wrong thoughts," said William Holden of Sophia Loren, his costar in 1958's *The Key*. Decades later, men are still thinking wrong thoughts, but women wonder how Loren, now in her 60s, maintains her legendary looks. The Italian star insists she has never gone under the knife, attributing her appearance to "rest, good thoughts and exercise." Family helps, too. As a 16-year-old beauty pageant contestant she met future husband Carlo Ponti, with whom she has two sons. What would put a smile on that extraordinary face? "I want to be a grandmother," she says. "But I want to be the sexiest grandmother in the world."

SOPHIA LOREN
TONY COSTA
1991

KATHARINE HEPBURN
JOHN BRYSON 1990

Serve Yourself

If Katharine Hepburn were a cocktail, the recipe would require one part sophistication, two parts feisty feminism plus a dash of reclusiveness. A self-described "aggressive, self-involved mutt," the four-time Oscar-winner (*Morning Glory, Guess Who's Coming to Dinner, The Lion in Winter* and *On Golden Pond*) lives alone (aside from staff) in Fenwick, Connecticut. There, in more vigorous days (she was 83 in this picture), Hepburn swam in Long Island Sound and scampered around the tennis court, allowing herself "any number of bounces."

Powerful Links

She's from Rye, New York. He's from Milton, Massachusetts, but grew up in Greenwich, Connecticut. Married in 1945, they've lived in Houston, Beijing, Maine and, of course, Washington, D.C. But for the globalist Bushes, home is where the golf bag is. In this case it was Nashville, where they snuck in a round before hosting a charity hoe-down to celebrate their golden anniversary. Nearly 4,000 of the Bushes' closest friends attended the fête at the Grand Ole Opry, including Vince Gill, Loretta Lynn and Delta Burke. Asked how they made it to the half-century mark, the former President credited "family and blessings in our life." His First Lady espoused her own theory. "He had," she suggested, "a great wife."

BARBARA & GEORGE BUSH
CHRISTOPHER LITTLE
1995

Diff'rent Strokes

After Gerald Ford tumbled down a few slippery airplane steps, the press corps and *Saturday Night Live*'s Chevy Chase cast him as an accident-prone oaf. In fact, Ford was one of the nation's most athletic public figures, having been voted MVP of the University of Michigan football team his senior year. Indeed, Ford turned down a chance to turn pro, opting instead to play a more bruising game, politics, and made it all the way to the White House pool.

GERALD FORD
DICK SWANSON
1976

Slam Dunk

Dennis Rodman may have floated beatifically in his San Antonio pool, but on the basketball court he was ferocious. Though small for NBA forwards (6'8"), he often led the league in rebounds, not to mention fines for insubordination. Dennis the Menace went after tabloid headlines as if they were a loose ball, cross-dressed in public, had a sensationally short marriage to actress Carmen Electra, got dropped by the Dallas Mavericks and likened himself to Michael Jordan but "on the flip side."

DENNIS RODMAN
HARRY BENSON
1995

BARRY WHITE
MARK SENNET 1995

Marine Dream With
his eight children (by two marriages and a
relationship) mostly scattered, crooner Barry
White settled into a Vegas mansion with
a 500-gallon saltwater aquarium and over
the years some $200,000 in fish. Which
was not to say he was lonely or melan-
choly. As White put it, "I'm probably the
happiest being you'll sit with in your life."

JESSICA SIMPSON DOROTHY LOW 2000

Makin' a Splash

A squeaky-clean image hasn't hurt the career of pop princess Jessica Simpson. The daughter of a Baptist minister, Simpson preaches premarital abstinence in interviews as well as in ballads like "Heart of Innocence"—a tribute to her apparently patient beau, Nick Lachey of the band 98°.

By Any Other Name
Born Roseanne Barr, she married Pentland, then Arnold, then Thomas. On the road to larger-than-life fame, she stopped using a last name altogether. Her eponymous sitcom was the first since Cosby's to hit Nielsen's No. 1 spot in its first season. In 1989 Roseanne revealed in her autobiography, *My Life as a Woman,* that her career impetus was a difficult upbringing. "I wouldn't be making a lot of money and be very happy now," she wrote, "if I had grown up content and sheltered." When her series ended in 1997, she morphed into a talk show host, only to get whupped in the ratings by daytime yak's reigning and sunnier Rosie.

ROSEANNE
TONY COSTA
1989

Mr. Clean
"I might as well ride in luxury," said Larry Flynt of his gold-plated wheelchair, a necessity since becoming paralyzed in a 1978 shooting. Indeed the once-poverty-stricken high school dropout from Kentucky surrounded his Hollywood home with over-the-top displays including a forest of Tiffany lamps. Having built an empire on the porn mag *Hustler,* Flynt, a father of three, also published such mainstream fare as *PC Laptop Computer* and *Maternity Fashion & Beauty,* which once—to her dismay after she discovered the ownership—put Kathie Lee Gifford on the cover.

LARRY FLYNT
DAVID STRICK
1993

Feel the Burn(out)

Once Gloria Steinem binned her boyfriend (real estate developer and publisher Mort Zuckerman), survived breast cancer and sold *Ms.* magazine, the feminist bible she cofounded and personified, it was time to focus on herself. Steinem cut back her busy lecture schedule and took up yoga (practicing here in the Manhattan duplex that she shares with her cat Magritte). Self-reflection, she decided, was "the next step" in the women's movement. "You can't do the external without the internal."

GLORIA STEINEM
LORI GRINKER
1992

The Eyes Have It

In *All About Eve,* Bette Davis (in L.A. two years before her death) mused in her smoky voice, "So many people know me. Except me. I wish someone would tell me about me." She could have done, however, without her daughter's scathing memoir about her inadequacy as a mother. And Davis herself conceded that after four divorces, she was "a failure as a wife." But she was a rare actress. When the Kennedy Center asked her to suggest possible honorees, Davis gave a customarily cocky reply: "Me."

BETTE DAVIS
FRANCOIS LEHR
1987

Comic Relief

If a sense of humor is truly a great aphrodisiac, then these are a few of the sexiest men and women alive

DAVID LETTERMAN
CHRISTOPHER LITTLE 1993

All Heart His irreverent take on the late-night talk format made David Letterman a hero of the up-past-Carson crowd, and for 11 years he delivered non sequiturs as if they were finely wrought punch lines. When Johnny retired in 1993, Letterman considered himself the natural successor, only to have NBC anoint Jay Leno. Letterman moved to CBS, taking with him those fans who preferred his sharper edge. His legions stood by him again in 2000 when the comic underwent a quintuple heart bypass. After only a few weeks he returned, grateful for his life but happily unmellowed by the melodrama of it all.

Talk to the Hand

A very tall and equally shy man, Jim Henson found it easier to communicate with society through a green felt amphibian. In 1969, Kermit the Frog (along with Big Bird and Cookie Monster) landed on a groundbreaking educational TV series, *Sesame Street.* Later, Henson's *Muppet Show* unleashed entertainment's premiere porcine sex symbol, Miss Piggy, drawing 235 million viewers and spinning off several films.

JIM HENSON
THE JIM HENSON
COMPANY
1985

Even with success, Henson deferred to the frog. After an interview he was likely to report, "I was terrible, but Kermit was great." Always dreaming up new creatures and venues for them, Henson, a father of five himself, was struck by pneumonia in 1990, and lost to the world at 53.

MARTIN SHORT
RAEANNE RUBENSTEIN 1984

Little Big Man

"Pat Sajak, a very decent fellow, I must say . . ." It hardly had the catchphrase potential of Billy Crystal's "You look mahvelous," but the line and the character, a geek named Ed Grimley, made Martin Short a star in his one season on *Saturday Night Live*. He would leave for films, and his first love, Broadway, collecting a Tony in 1999 for *Little Me*.

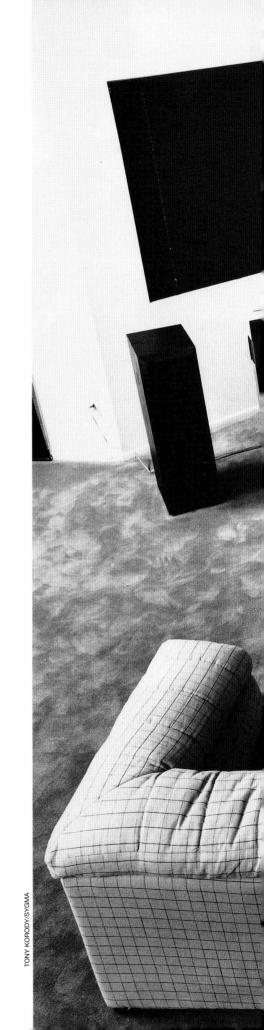

Like, Cosmo, Man

Two canceled series in a row (*Fridays* and *Marblehead Manor*) might have some actors looking for vocational guidance. But not Michael Richards. At an audition for a new show, titled *The Seinfeld Chronicles,* he read his lines standing on his head. But the show's star, Jerry Seinfeld, was already a fan and cast him as his flaky neighbor, Cosmo Kramer. With success, Richards sought new ways to enlarge his perspective. He did his best thinking, he said, while snorkeling at the bottom of his San Fernando Valley pool.

MICHAEL RICHARDS
STEVE LABADESSA
1993

TONY KORODY/SYGMA

Master of His Domain

When he finally became a casino headliner, stand-up Jerry Seinfeld was just glad to stop performing "at 2 a.m. to three people putting on their coats." Back in 1988, he couldn't foresee the breakthrough that lay ahead. His sitcom started slowly the following year, but after nine seasons, his annual take hit $90 million, and he ended his eponymous epoch before 76 million viewers.

Last Laugh

If nervous titters count, then Andy Kaufman broke up every audience he faced. Though he loved to make people uncomfortable—he once slept onstage for 10 minutes—he also craved adoration, and was hurt when viewers voted him off *Saturday Night Live* in a call-in poll. Most famous for playing *Taxi*'s Latke, a sweet-natured mechanic of indeterminate foreign origin, he buried that persona when the show went off the air, and built a new one: a female-wrestling boor. If fans were offended, it was only because they didn't get the joke. When his death from cancer hit the news in 1984, some figured he was pulling their leg yet again. But it was true: He was gone at age 35.

**ANDY
KAUFMAN**
MADDY MILLER
1979

Fabio vs. the Reege

When romance cover boy Fabio visited *Live with Regis & Kathie Lee,* the hosts staged a novel pose. (Or maybe Philbin felt the need to play chaperone in case Gifford's kid, Cody, tuned in; Cassidy wasn't born yet.) After 15 years of similarly caffeinated antics, Gifford announced she would leave the show in 2000, and Philbin moonlighted lucratively on *Who Wants to Be a Millionaire.* Fabio, meanwhile, announced his search for a signora. Tough luck that Gifford stuck by momentarily straying husband Frank; she and Fab made a cute couple.

REGIS PHILBIN, FABIO & KATHIE LEE GIFFORD
STEVE FRIEDMAN
1992

Horseplay Whether he's chasing impish Roberto Benigni with a giant net or deliberately mistaking the filmmaking Coen brothers for the murdering Menendez boys, emcee extraordinaire Billy Crystal—here jawing on the streets of his native New York City—makes the annual Academy Awards marathon unbridled and somehow bearable. "You think of the best lines backstage," says Crystal, who has hosted the show seven times (second only to Bob Hope's 17). Though a cool conqueror of the Catskills and romantic comedy (*When Harry Met Sally*), Crystal admits to pre-Oscar nightmares: "There's enormous pressure being live for three and a half hours in front of the world. The world's a tough room."

BILLY CRYSTAL
LAWRENCE
SCHWARTZWALD
1993

No Sucker

Life seemed as sweet as a lollipop for Eddie Murphy when he began electrifying audiences at 19 on *Saturday Night Live* with his less than worshipful impressions. Then he morphed into a movie star in *48HRS, Trading Places* and *Beverly Hills Cop,* only to nearly succumb to an ego implosion, as he hung with a thuggish entourage and cut music albums that misfired. "You get born only once in this business, but you can die over and over again," he reckoned. "But then you come back." Murphy rebounded with a vengeance as the humble heavy-

EDDIE MURPHY
MIMI COTTER
1982

weight Sherman Klump (and family) in the remake of *The Nutty Professor.*

Barr Tender

John Goodman likens toiling as an unknown actor in New York City to plunging into "a Waring Blender set for puree." But the bulky St. Louis native somehow got out intact and found fame portraying Dan Connor, Roseanne's poker-and-guitar-playing helpmate on her hit blue-collar sitcom. "People are starting to put my face with my name," marveled the self-deprecating new star, "instead of think-

JOHN GOODMAN
STEPHEN ELLISON 1988

ing I'm either somebody they went to high school with or did time with."

Bug Off
"Any good humor is sophomoric. Sophomoric is the liberal word for funny," said Michael O'Donoghue, the mad mind behind some of *Saturday Night Live*'s funniest and raunchiest early bits. This gag shot aside, pest control for him was extraneous chatter to distract network censors during rehearsal of dicey lines.

MICHAEL O'DONOGHUE
MIMI COTTER
1979

He was just 54 when he died of a brain hemorrhage in 1994.

Great Escape
Long before Tim Allen portrayed a cutup with a circular saw on *Home Improvement* and a Captain Kirk clone in the film *Galaxy Quest,* he played to a tougher crowd while serving time on a cocaine conviction at Minnesota's Sandstone Correctional Institution. "Humor was the only defense I had," he remembers. "Two minutes after I was there I started babbling." A dozen years following his parole, he had turned his time in stir and

TIM ALLEN
JONATHAN EXLEY
1992

other memories into a 1994 bestseller, *Don't Stand Too Close to a Naked Man.*

JONATHAN EXLEY/LIAISON AGENCY

CAMRYN MANHEIM
FRANK VERONSKY 1999

Big Deal Once promised a puppy by her parents if she would drop a few pounds, Camryn Manheim proved to them —and to size-obsessed casting directors—that large can be lovely. She won a 1998 Emmy for her brassy portrayal of lawyer Ellenor Frutt on *The Practice*, and joyfully dedicated it to "all the fat girls."

CLARA PELLER MARK SENNET 1984

Hamburger Helper

Known for her lungs rather than her buns, Wendy's pitchwoman Clara Peller huffed her way into the nation's heart, bellowing, "Where's the beef?" Raising sales 32 percent and becoming part of the national lexicon, the slogan was pilfered during the 1984 Democratic presidential primary by Walter Mondale to mock challenger Gary Hart. Marveled the 4'10" Peller before her death at 86 in 1987: "I didn't know I'd get that big."

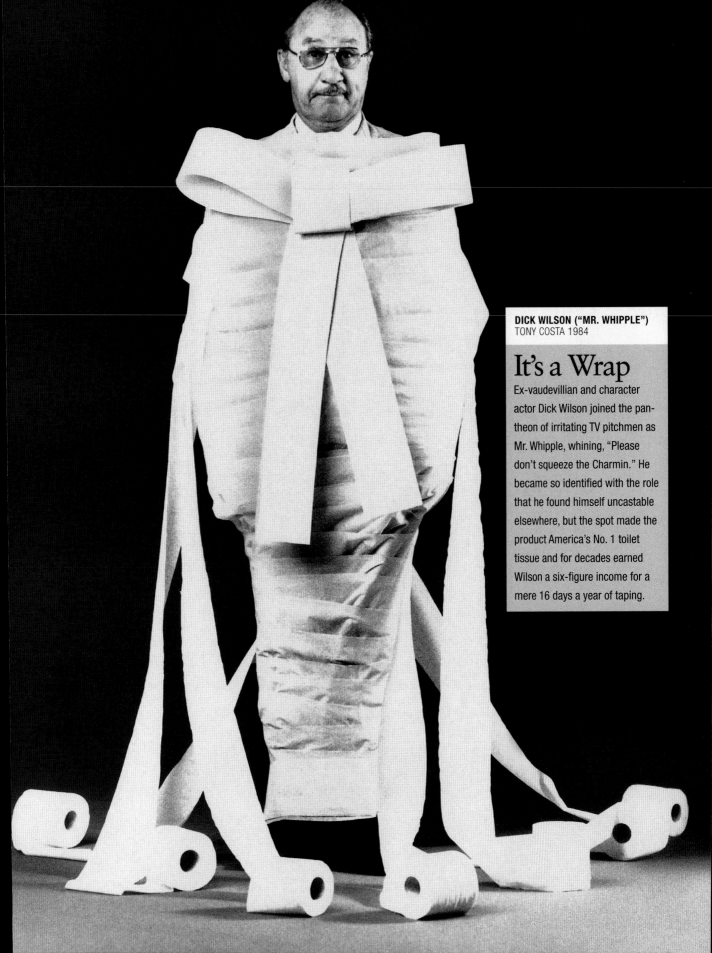

DICK WILSON ("MR. WHIPPLE")
TONY COSTA 1984

It's a Wrap

Ex-vaudevillian and character actor Dick Wilson joined the pantheon of irritating TV pitchmen as Mr. Whipple, whining, "Please don't squeeze the Charmin." He became so identified with the role that he found himself uncastable elsewhere, but the spot made the product America's No. 1 toilet tissue and for decades earned Wilson a six-figure income for a mere 16 days a year of taping.

FAMILY TIES

Celebrity theory of relativity: You can pick your stylist, stage name and spouse but not your kin

Panned Parenthood

"I'm supposed to have had more men than most people change underwear," said Tanya Tucker, who did nab as many tabloid headlines as Nashville hits. When she settled into motherhood, she kept daughter Presley and son Grayson on her palatial Tennessee spread during a seven-year long-distance romance with their father, actor Ben Reed, who lived in California. When the conservative country-music press criticized the arrangement, Tucker responded, "I didn't set out to be an example; I just wanted children. They are no mistake." Ultimately the relationship ended, and she won custody. In 1999 Tucker and her new fiancé, songwriter Jerry Laseter, expanded the brood with daughter Layla.

TANYA & GRAYSON TUCKER
HARRY BENSON
1994

Secret Love

Rumors that John F. Kennedy Jr. and Carolyn Bessette were engaged were still emerging when the couple snuck away to an intimate wedding in a chapel built by freed slaves on Georgia's tiny Cumberland Island. Witnessed by 40 loved ones, the candlelit ceremony would have made Kennedy's mother, Jacqueline, proud for its elegance and lack of media coverage.

**JOHN & CAROLYN
KENNEDY**
DENIS REGGIE
1996

"It was very important for us to conduct this in a private, prayerful and meaningful way," said the groom. He was, he said, "the happiest man alive." By the time word got out of the union, the new Mr. and Mrs. Kennedy had jetted off to their honeymoon in, it was only later revealed, Turkey.

Counter Intelligence

When she dropped by her father Vernon's general store in Nashville, Oprah Winfrey was already a star. But as a child, she had been shuffled between relatives, and sexually abused by a cousin. Her way out was reading. After college—which she says she hated—she got into broadcasting. Charismatic, but deemed too emotional for the news, she soon had a talk show. Yet despite her success on TV, she never forgot her debt to literature and launched the nation's biggest book club, making millionaires of favorite authors, and avid readers of some otherwise couched potatoes.

OPRAH & VERNON WINFREY
HARRY BENSON
1987

PRINCESS DIANA & WILLIAM
TIM GRAHAM 1982

His Highness Childbirth was
almost easier for Diana than settling on a name, and
for days the boy was called simply Baby Wales. His
father had argued for Arthur. Yet Mom prevailed with
William, though she soon bestowed a new title on
the precocious future king: "mini tornado."

Just Mum

In her lifetime, much of the world viewed Diana, Princess of Wales, as the heroine of a fairy tale gone wrong. But to sons William and Harry (here at ages 7 and 4) she was a pretty regular mom. She took part in school events, played the games the boys loved and raised them in a hands-on way unfamiliar to their royal relatives. When she died in 1997, her casket bore a handwritten note addressed simply to "Mummy."

Putting on a Happy Face

For eight years mother-daughter singers Naomi and Wynonna Judd had been traveling and performing together. But this trip was different. Naomi had been diagnosed with a sometimes fatal form of hepatitis, and the tour was announced as her last. Each night on the Juddmobile (below), Naomi felt "totally exhausted, numb." Wynonna, who described her mom as "a broken doll," fretted about going solo. But fans embraced her, and she became a star in her own right. The ultimate satisfaction came on New Year's Eve, 1999, when the Judds played a reunion concert. "She's back," said Wynonna. "And it is very humbling."

NAOMI & WYNONNA JUDD
CHRISTOPHER LITTLE
1991

Keys to the Kingdom

Recording what would be his last album, John Lennon seemed to be saying, "Someday, son, all this will be yours." Later that year, Lennon, 40, was killed outside their New York City apartment. Sean, only four, was too young for the press to speculate whether he would continue his dad's musical legacy—half brother Julian got that scrutiny. There were similarities, however, in the way Sean deflected media inquiries with humor, as in his dry comment "I like it best when reporters ask, 'Do you think it's time to be going?'" Influenced also by his mother, Yoko Ono, Sean did eventually make music his career, titling his 1998 debut album *Into the Sun.*

JOHN & SEAN LENNON
ALLAN TANNENBAUM
1980

Model Mom
Pregnancy agreed with 20-year-old Niki Taylor, a model from age 13. Though naturally thin, the six-foot beauty had always watched her weight. But when she and then husband Matt Martinez, a football coach, learned she was eating for three, she rejoiced at the prospect of throwing out the rice cakes. "I ate meat and potatoes every night," she said happily. At their arrival, twins Hunter (left) and Jake each weighed a healthy seven pounds—though Mom had put on 70. Three months later Taylor had trimmed down and hit the runways in Paris, but with a difference. "I have hips now," she exulted. "It makes me more sexy."

NIKI TAYLOR & TWINS
FRANK VERONSKY
1997

The Long Run

When she ran, time seemed to stand still for Florence Griffith-Joyner, the Fastest Woman on Earth at the 1988 Seoul Olympics. When FloJo died 10 years later of a brain seizure, the clock stopped in the home she had shared with husband Al Joyner and daughter Mary. Joyner wouldn't sleep in the couple's bedroom until he had remodeled it. For a while he wouldn't let anyone else clean it. And, a track star himself, he quit training for the triple jump. It took his daughter, "eight going on 28," he said, to get him through the grieving and to start again. Mary, who herself began running after her mother's death, said, "Daddy, Momma would want you to do it, and so do I."

AL & MARY JOYNER
NEAL PRESTON
1999

The Trouble with Kids

Sure, their gilded Encino, California, home was bought with money their children earned, and Joe and Katherine Jackson are proud of their singing kids—Michael, Janet, Marlon, Tito, Jermaine, Jackie and LaToya. But they're also worried about them. After the lucrative Jackson 5 act broke up, some of its members were hurting for cash. Michael, who clearly was not, lived in defiant seclusion from his family and published a book charging mistreatment as a child. Three of the younger Jacksons saw their marriages fall apart. Janet, whose album *Control*

**KATHERINE &
JOE JACKSON**
HARRY BENSON
1988

marked her personal breakout, fired Dad as her manager. And LaToya let a felonious boyfriend steer her fleeting career. "The problems," maintained patriarch Joe Jackson, "all developed after the children turned 18 and started making decisions on their own."

Sealed with a Kiss

When this photograph was taken, in Little Rock, Arkansas, Gov. Bill Clinton was a few days away from becoming his party's nominee for President. Even then, with the name Gennifer Flowers common coin, Americans wondered what pact or chemistry kept the Clintons whole. Eight years later, the question has yielded no simple answers. They are buddies, they are battlers for and with each other, they are proud and loving parents, they are an open wound and a closed book. "The only people who count in any marriage are the two that are in it," the First Lady said in 1998. "We know everything there is to know about each other, and we understand and accept and love each other." In 1997 Bill told PEOPLE that for 20 years their lives had been "basically driven by my political career. So I figure now I owe her 20 years." Win or lose in her New York run for Senate, Hillary may have already begun collecting.

BILL & HILLARY CLINTON
HARRY BENSON
1992

Drama Queens

After the divorce of her parents, Janet Leigh and Tony Curtis, Jamie, then 3, and her sister Kelly went to live with Leigh. "I remember putting on shows in the basement," she said. "Mom let us children stay children." As a grown-up, playacting became real as she followed in her folks' footsteps. About that time Curtis started to reconnect with her mostly absentee dad. Now a mom of two herself, she talks to both parents every week, and family takes precedence over work. "I'd love to not live my life up on a movie screen," she says.

JAMIE LEE CURTIS & JANET LEIGH
KEN REGAN
1994

KEN REGAN/CAMERA 5

Picture Perfect

"This is how I hoped my life would be," said Valerie Bertinelli, married to rocker Eddie Van Halen and mother to Wolfgang, then 5. But getting to that happy place wasn't so easy. The former *One Day at a Time* star went through long courses of therapy, as did her hard-partying husband. And though always in demand for TV movies, she hated being away from Wolfie, noting, "I'd rather spend time with him than anything else."

VALERIE BERTINELLI & WOLFGANG VAN HALEN
NEAL PRESTON
1997

THE TWO MRS. VON FURSTENBERG
TODD FRANCE 1998

Prints Charming

Forget what you think about mothers-in-law. Diane Von Furstenberg broke the you're-not-good-enough-for-my-son mold by embracing daughter-in-law Alexandra and putting her to work. Alexandra, who began as an intern, helped hubby's mom reenvision her signature wrap dress for its 20th anniversary. Which proves that she has good taste in guys—and in garb.

Her Father's Eyes

For 11 years, Canadian-born bandleader Paul Shaffer was dedicated to David Letterman, moving with him from NBC to CBS. His personal life, however, lacked that continuity. He and girlfriend Cathy Vasapoli met in the late 1970s but couldn't commit. "We were always breaking up, getting back together and breaking up again," he explained. "After a two-year separation, I had to admit she was the girl for me." In 1990, three years after they married, the Shaffers welcomed a daughter, Lily. "She gets her looks, fortunately, from her mother," said Shaffer. But her taste in shades is definitely Dad's.

PAUL & LILY SHAFFER
KIMBERLY BUTLER
1993

Ladies' Man

"If I had sons, I'd be a feminist whose sons are feminists," said Alan Alda, in response to the charge that his equal-opportunity outlook was shaped by his photographer wife, Arlene (left), and three daughters. (Beatrice and Elizabeth, above, were actresses; Eve was away at school during this shoot in New York City's Central Park.) During his nine seasons playing Hawkeye Pierce on *M*A*S*H*, Alda kept his family in the east and famously commuted home every weekend. In the Hollywood community, Alda was known as the sensitive guy who once sent back a sexist script with a note saying, "I won't act in this, but if you tell me when it's opening, I'll picket."

THE ALDA FAMILY
RAEANNE
RUBENSTEIN
1981

California Girls

Chynna Phillips (left), daughter of Mama Michelle and Papa John, and Carnie Wilson (middle) and her sister Wendy, whose dad is Beach Boy Brian, attended the same private schools and

WILSON PHILLIPS
ROB KINMONTH
1990

watched their folks divorce. In 1990, they tried to build on their families' legacies with a group, and their catchy harmonies got them a hit single with "Hold On." The trio didn't, though. Wilson Phillips broke up after three years.

Life Lessons

Born 12 years apart to different moms, step-siblings Jason Alexander and Karen Van Horn were not that close when he was launching a theater career in New York and she was overseas with her then husband in the military. "I was totally self-absorbed," he says. But they grew together during his *Seinfeld* years, when she had settled in Houston. And their bond became ever stronger after Van Horn was diag-

JASON ALEXANDER & KAREN VAN HORN
DEBORAH FEINGOLD
1996

nosed with life-threatening scleroderma. "He has taught me to see humor in things," she says. From her, Alexander says he has learned to "be more involved with what the quality of life is all about."

Close to You

"We are each other's best friend," said Karen Carpenter of her brother and bandmate, Richard. Their pretty but bland sound was ubiqui-ous on 1970s radio, making both siblings rich, but neither very happy. On the release of their 17th album, both were between relationships and hoping to find the love they often sang about. But in 1983 Karen, 33, died of a heart attack caused by anorexia. Since then, Richard has put out solo albums and collaborations with friends

KAREN & RICHARD CARPENTER
STEVE SHAPIRO
1976

like Dionne Warwick. But none were as suc-cessful as those with his beloved sister.

Strange Bedfellows

Must have been "That Old Black Magic" that united chanteuse Margaret Whiting and the bisexual porn star Jack Wrangler. Cupid struck the unlikely couple after a chance encounter at a nightclub. Wrangler admitted having "limited" experience with women, but as he recalled it, "I looked over [and] there she was with the hair, the furs, and the big gestures. I thought, 'Boy, now *that's* New York. That's glamour.'" She, in turn, was enticed by his "humor, taste and imagination." So at ages 54 and 32, they settled into a Manhattan pad, decorated with her gold records and his cheesecake shots. "There's so much unhappiness in the world," pointed out Whiting. "If you can find someone who makes you happy, then c'mon, who cares?"

MARGARET WHITING
& JACK WRANGLER
HARRY BENSON
1987

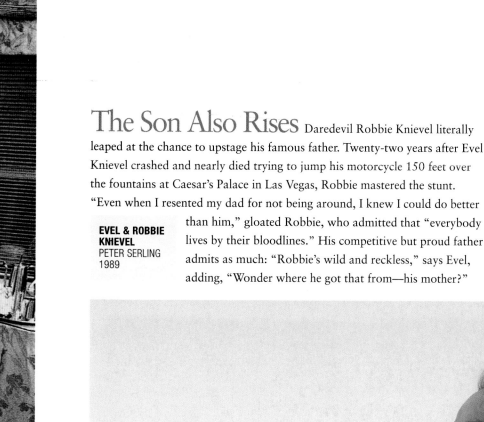

The Son Also Rises

Daredevil Robbie Knievel literally leaped at the chance to upstage his famous father. Twenty-two years after Evel Knievel crashed and nearly died trying to jump his motorcycle 150 feet over the fountains at Caesar's Palace in Las Vegas, Robbie mastered the stunt. "Even when I resented my dad for not being around, I knew I could do better than him," gloated Robbie, who admitted that "everybody lives by their bloodlines." His competitive but proud father admits as much: "Robbie's wild and reckless," says Evel, adding, "Wonder where he got that from—his mother?"

EVEL & ROBBIE KNIEVEL
PETER SERLING
1989

THE DOUGLASES TONY COSTA 1980

Champs
Life went swimmingly for Kirk and Anne Douglas, here paddling in their Palm Springs pool, until the dimpled one suffered a 1997 stroke. During his rehab, she took on the role of cheerleader. "Anne," he says, "fills a tremendous void in my life."

THE GIFFORDS CHRISTOPHER LITTLE 1990

Kid Talk
"The most wonderful thing you can share is a baby," said football's Frank Gifford. Wife Kathie Lee took those words to heart, making a TV career out of going public about son Cody (pictured), his kid sister Cassidy and other family matters.

THE ESTEFANS
ACEY HARPER 1991

Tune-Up
Gloria Estefan's two loves—music and husband Emilio—helped her recover from a vertebrae-shattering tour bus accident and a subsequent bout of lyricist's block. Her husband's feat was to coax her back into their Miami studio. "Emilio played 'Coming Out of the Dark,'" remembers Estefan, "and everything just tumbled out."

MARK SENNET/REFLEX

Cher Alike "If Michelangelo painted in Caesar's Palace, would that make it any less art?" demanded Cher, well aware that her gaudy Vegas act made it hard to take seriously her stunning breakthrough film *Silkwood*. At home, she was raising Chastity Bono, then 14, and Elijah, 9, the son from her brief marriage to rocker Gregg Allman. Explaining Gregg's absence, she told Elijah that Dad was busy. "Mother," responded the boy, clearly as perceptive as Mom, "he's not too busy to pick up the telephone."

CHER & ELIJAH ALLMAN
MARK SENNET
1984

Pianissimo "With female children, you want to try to teach them early to understand men," advised Paul McCartney, an avowed ladies' man until he met wife Linda Eastman, and also father of three girls. (Son James came later.) The youngest, Stella, had Mom's blond hair, and a passing interest in music when Pop was at the piano. But inspired perhaps by those old Nehru jackets in the closet, her interest turned to fashion, and at 26 she replaced Karl Lagerfeld as the head designer at Chloe.

PAUL & STELLA McCARTNEY
HARRY BENSON
1975

That's Our Boy

"Did he write about how we were in the theater once and I told him to go into the corner and relieve himself of his gas?" asked Ben Stern. Apparently Ben was among the last people in America to read *Private Parts,* his son Howard's megaselling memoir. "He developed a lot of gas as a child," offered the retired engineer, removing any doubt of the potty-mouthed radio host's lineage. The family's humor aside, Howard had a typical Long Island suburban upbringing, and tried to re-create it for his three daughters with wife Alison (second from right, with Ben, Stern's mother Ray and his sister Ellen). But the couple separated after 21 years in 1999. "I'm here," he announced on his first show after the split. "All broads, please call."

THE STERN FAMILY
ANDREW BRUSSO
1993

Pappy Trails

A lot of kids grew up in the 1950s with Roy Rogers lunchboxes and pajamas and Double R logos on their cowboy boots. Dusty Rogers had that and more: Roy Rogers was his pa. Yet, as he reflected (here at 40, visiting his old room), "when I was a kid, I wondered what in the world was so exciting about this guy." His mother, Grace Wilkins, died shortly after giving birth to Dusty; Rogers' second wife, Dale Evans, is the woman he called Mom. After high school, Dusty toyed with following in his folks' footsteps, but Dad insisted he get a "good job." Though he did make two films, Dusty wound up a building contractor. Roy rode off into the sunset in 1998 at 86.

ROY & DUSTY ROGERS
MARK SENNET
1987

On THE JOB

What begins with the genes, a flight of genius and demonic drive ends with Lights! Camera! Acclaim!

Crossover Cowboy

As country-and-western's emissary to the pop world, Garth Brooks practices diplomacy on tour (200 nights a year), crooning, twirling like a tumbleweed in a tornado, two-stepping and, on occasion, smashing guitars. He grew up "downright poor," says his bassist and half sister Betsy, and hurled the javelin on scholarship at Oklahoma State. Indeed, his road manager Mick Weber believes his "intensity comes from athletics. Once he hits the stage, it's game day." Brooks, a once-roving but now stably married dad of three, comes up with a slightly different metaphor for his motivation in the spotlight: It's like making "love with my music in front of women."

GARTH BROOKS
FRANK
MICELOTTA
1991

Breaking Away

When the Prince and Princess of Wales visited the London set of the James Bond movie *The Living Daylights,* Charles invited Diana to knock the pretend daylights out of him with a spun-sugar prop bottle he had been handed. "I can't, I can't," she protested. "I would never be able to forget it." But the Prince persisted, and finally Diana, who had long known about his philandering with Camilla Parker Bowles (and had not yet strayed herself), smashingly obliged him. "That'll have to last you another 10 years," Charles cracked. In a way, it did. Their divorce became final exactly a decade later. Diana's settlement included $23 million cash, $30 million in jewelry and her nine-room pad in Kensington Palace.

DIANA & CHARLES
ALPHA/GLOBE
1986

ALAN SHELDON/TIGRESS/MERIDIAN/WNET

Beauty and the Beast
While shooting an English TV documentary on the vanishing habitat of the Indonesian orangutan, Julia Roberts insisted on camping in the jungle to observe the primates at close range. She bonded easily with one baby, accepting "a nice little love bite on the ear." But her encounter with a 400-pound adult male named Kusasi ended with filmmaker Nigel Cole prying the animal's massive mitts from her neck. Ben Bratt, the alpha male in Roberts' life, later viewed the tape, commenting, "Even though I knew she was going to be fine . . . a beast of a few hundred pounds with a hand that can crush walnuts wrapped around her throat . . . Yeah, there was need for a little concern."

JULIA ROBERTS
ALAN SHELDON
1998

JOHN TRAVOLTA
JIM McHUGH 1983

Tights End Playing Tony Manero in *Saturday Night Fever* earned John Travolta an Oscar nomination and a second blockbuster, *Grease.* Then he made a few poor moves, turning down *American Gigolo* and *An Officer and a Gentleman.* Bulking up for Sly Stallone's 1984 *Fever* sequel, *Staying Alive* (here), he proved he was not just a peacock but a swan.

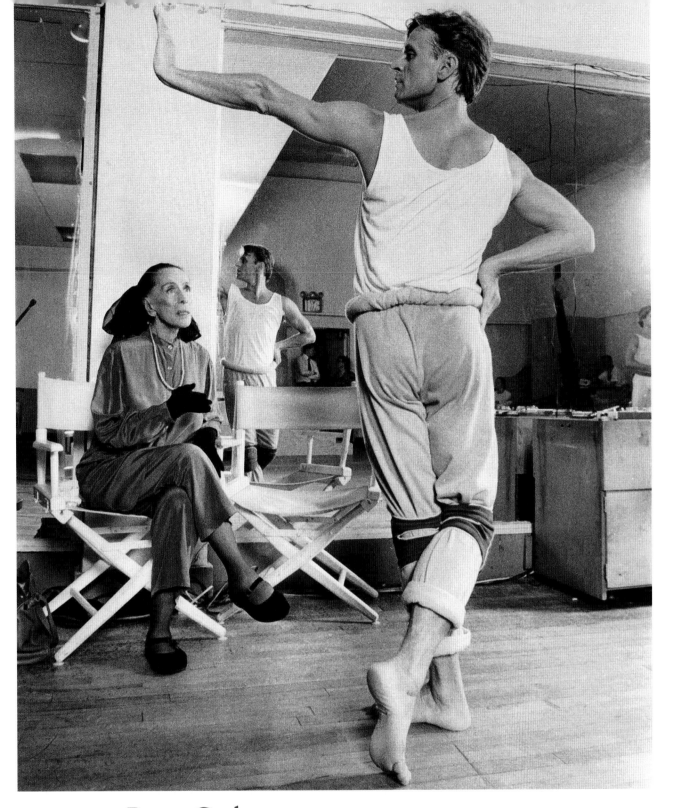

Barre Code

Two terpsichorean legends, equally hot-blooded, can make for one fraught pas de deux. Mikhail Baryshnikov, at 41, had retired as head of American Ballet Theater but had not lost the gifts that had made him one of the greatest dancers of the century. Modern-dance pioneer Martha Graham, famous for slapping, berating and even biting her dancers, took a gentler tack with Misha in reworking her 1938 *American Document* for him. Graham, who stopped performing at age 76, said at 95, "I would still love to dance very much." She died a year later, in 1991, still choreographing.

MARTHA GRAHAM & MIKHAIL BARYSHNIKOV
MARTHA SWOPE
1989

Speed Bump

For years, Macaulay Culkin cornered the market on mischievous cute, tormenting bumbling burglars in the *Home Alone* films and riding to the rescue of *My Girl* (being shot below). But Culkin's act got old before he did. The actor, who married his high school sweetheart, actress Rachel Miner, at 17, hasn't worked since puberty—and doesn't need to. This real-life Richie Rich gained access to his $17 million fortune when he turned 18.

MACAULAY CULKIN
ACEY HARPER
1991

Am Misbehaving

Precocious success brought the threat of early flameout to theater scion Drew Barrymore. Here matched with Stephen King at the Maine premiere of *Firestarter* (he wrote the novel, she acted), Barrymore started smoking cigarettes that same year at 9, got into pot by 10 and snorted cocaine soon after. Thanks to stints in rehab, Barrymore grew into maturer roles in Wes Craven's *Scream* and Woody Allen's *Everybody Says I Love You*. Suggested *Scream*'s producer Cary Woods: "Drew lives in dog years."

DREW BARRYMORE & STEPHEN KING
MIMI COTTER
1984

Lord of the Ring

No, he wasn't trying to remind himself of the script. Hulk Hogan was praying before a match. A 6'6", 290-pound former rock bass player, Terry Mollea (as he was born) helped propel pro wrestling from a sideshow to the center ring of the entertainment circus. In the process, the TV ratings and pay-per-view grosses ballooned, and Hogan became the spectacle's first million-dollar man, endorsing everything from kids' vitamins to Right Guard deodorant. The Hulkster even talked about running for President but got beaten to the political punch by Jesse "The Body" Ventura.

HULK HOGAN
ACEY HARPER
1992

PAUL PRUDHOMME RAEANNE RUBENSTEIN 1985

Bayou Guru Armed with native spices, a hot skillet and a Nawlins drawl thick as gumbo, Paul Prudhomme, the 13th child of sharecroppers, nearly endangered a species with his delectable blackened redfish and turned foodie America on to a new cuisine. "Cajun," boomed the 400-pound author and restaurateur, "makes you happy."

All That Glitters

When they wanted to turn heads on Oscar or other nights, many of Hollywood's most out-front stars turned themselves over to Bob Mackie (left, with business partner Ray Aghayan). But by the early 1990s, the guru of glitz had lost a son to AIDS, seen his New York couture house founder and gotten loans from clients like Cher and Carol Burnett (not to mention the Gambino crime family). "The clothes are clean," said the designer after a comeback in his native Los Angeles, "but the garment industry isn't always."

**BOB MACKIE &
RAY AGHAYAN**
STEVE SCHAPIRO
1975

So Suit Me!

It is impossible to overstate how Giorgio Armani's understated, deconstructed designs transformed fashion—as well as the look of countless celebrities. The Milan-based Armani counts Robert De Niro, Whoopi Goldberg, Eric Clapton, Jodie Foster and Billy Joel among his clients—and Michelle Pfeiffer as his muse. "She can bring to life even the simplest outfit," gushes Armani, whose mission, he says, is to help people "refine their style without having them become victims of fashion."

**GIORGIO ARMANI
& MODEL**
DAVID LEES
1979

Profit Motif

Dishing out free duds to folks who could afford them like Mick Jagger and Sean "Puffy" Combs, Tommy Hilfiger generated buzz for a preppy, patriotic line seen from the inner city to the campus to the country club. Set back by dyslexia, he himself never got past high school and was more distinguished as a marketeer than designer. "I'm proud to be an American," he declared, "and I think it shows in what I do."

TOMMY HILFIGER
THEO
WESTENBERGER
1997

Scare Tactics

Spookmeister R.L. Stine compares his books (like *Goosebumps*) to roller-coaster rides: "The story is fast, with lots of twists and turns—lots of screams. Then it lets you off safe and sound at the end." Each month, nearly 5 million young readers climb aboard, making him the U.S.'s best-read author.

R.L. STINE
THEO
WESTENBERGER
1995

"I might sell 30 million books this year," said Stine, who types with just one finger. "Of course," he added, "no one else writes 24 a year."

A Contender

Sylvester Stallone was Hollywood's poet laureate of pugilism not least because he steeped himself in his art and the sport. Between his third and fourth *Rocky* films, he became manager of a fledgling fighter named Lee Canalito (above, right). Sly called the seven-inches-taller heavyweight "an exact duplicate of what I would like to be if I could rebuild myself. He'll become everything I can't be." Canalito did hammer Sly when they sparred but, unlike Rocky, never took a title.

SYLVESTER STALLONE
NEIL LEIFER
1982

Side Man

The onscreen star of *Mo' Better Blues,* the fellow with the trumpet, was Denzel Washington. But the auteur who made the movie sing was director Spike Lee. To tell the story of a musician caught in a love triangle, Lee relied on his jazz composer dad, Bill, to write the score, and his sister Joie to play a music teacher. Working with family helped Lee keep the story true to the New York City milieu in which he grew up. Besides, he said, "I try not to work with actors who ask me, 'What's my motivation?'"

SPIKE LEE
MARIO RUIZ
1990

Tent Revival

"As a ringmaster, I am able to be somebody's brother, father, teacher and preacher," said Cal Dupree, who runs the action under the big top of the UniverSoul Circus, the first predominantly African-American troupe. Dupree and coproducer Cedric Walker, once music promoters who were unhappy with unwholesome fare in rap, sought a form of black entertainment for the whole family. Their traveling show employs 60 performers and brings commerce to the inner-city areas where they pitch their tent. His dream project? "A black theme park."

CAL DUPREE
JOHN STOREY
1997

G'night, Ma

After seven seasons and scores of family trauma (Grandpa's passing, John Boy's departure) on Walton's Mountain, Mother was leaving the cast. For her colleagues on the popular series, it was as wrenching as if a real family member had just decided to up and go. But Michael Learned, who played the Depression-era farm matriarch Olivia Walton, was tired of the weekly TV grind. Her farewell episode, however, was taped out of sequence. For had Olivia's final show been the star's last too, she said, "they could never get it on film. Too many tears."

THE WALTONS
JIM McHUGH
1979

STAR'S BEST FRIEND

Puppy Love "Dating," declared Pfeiffer in 1989, "is like a disaster." How could a woman so devastatingly gorgeous be so unlucky in love? After divorcing actor Peter Horton, she formed relationships with Val Kilmer and Fisher Stevens, but preferred spending evenings alone with her dogs Ben and Sasha (at right). "What makes me happy is to be loved, but it's hard to achieve." Easier was making her way in film, with a string of luminous turns from *Dangerous Liaisons* to *The Deep End of the Ocean*. The lonely beauty would eventually find a match in prolific TV producer David E. Kelley. They married in 1993, and soon Pfeiffer could admit, "I'm happy. You can definitely see it on my face."

MICHELLE PFEIFFER
BLAKE LITTLE
1989

In a fickle galaxy where you feel only as good as your last property, where is a beauty without her beast?

STEVE MARTIN HARRY BENSON 1980

Cat Nip
What kind of jerk serves kitty for lunch? After dining out on the success of his first film, *The Jerk,* Steve Martin soon traded the wild and crazy stuff for *Roxanne,* a clever take on Cyrano; a humorous play about Picasso; and highbrow pieces for *The New Yorker.* This year the American Museum of the Moving Image honored him with a retrospective of his inspired films. Goofy, with a side of smart.

FRAN DRESCHER
MARK SENNET 1989

Woof & Warp

Oh, that voice! Could anything grate on you more than the yap of Fran Drescher's Pomeranian? That year both Fran and Chester appeared in *Cadillac Man* (she as Robin Williams' girlfriend, he as her dog). Four years on, Drescher, and her equally captivating intonation, scored as *The Nanny* (CBS), proving that it isn't only silence that is golden.

MARK SENNET/REFLEX

Short Order His portrayal of a sauced but lovable millionaire in

Arthur heated up Dudley Moore's film career and gave the actor and pianist a fame
that, he said, "makes me feel nice and warm in my tummy." So did his offscreen love,
singer Susan Anton. The diminutive star (with Peke Kong) seemed to relish life as
much as his carefree alter ego did. But one sequel, two marriages and 18 years later,

**DUDLEY
MOORE**
MARK SENNET
1981

his life took a sobering turn when he was diagnosed with a pro-
gressive brain disease. His speech slurred by the malady, Moore
appeared at a 1999 benefit to bring music to hospitals. "It was
marvelous to be back onstage," he said. "Just wonderful."

RICK MORANIS & DAVE THOMAS
MADDY MILLER 1982

Funny, eh?

In response to a government requirement that Canadian TV shows include Canadian content, *SCTV*'s Rick Moranis (left) and Dave Thomas created the dim Canucks Bob and Doug McKenzie. Fueled by beer and back bacon, they became a cult hit (and, at their peak, posed with befurred PEOPLE editor Cutler Durkee). In 1999 the *SCTV* troupe reunited for one last show; the McKenzies live on in ads for Molson beer.

Pop Genes

A teenager when she met husband and bandmate Papa John Phillips, Mama Michelle was now raising Chynna, 10, alone and nurturing a solo career. (That year she cut a record and shot a lurid film about Rudolph Valentino.) She also predicted big things for her daughter, but wouldn't let her perform before turning 18. In the 1990s the elder Phillips settled into TV work, while Chynna co-founded the band Wilson Phillips, propelling the family name back up the charts to No. 1.

A Brave Face

A star for more than three decades when she published an autobiography in 1995, Mary Tyler Moore revealed details of her alcoholism and the loss of a son who accidentally shot himself. By then, contentedly married 11 years to third husband Robert Levine, a cardiologist, she found the strength to mine the difficult terrain of her personal history. "Little Mary, happy at last," assessed Moore (with basset Dudley). Five years later she revived her most famous — and famously upbeat—role, playing opposite Valerie Harper in the TV film *Mary and Rhoda.*

MARY TYLER MOORE
CHRISTOPHER LITTLE
1995

MARK SENNET/REFLEX

New Tricks

A veteran with Emmys for *Roots, Rich Man Poor Man* and *The Mary Tyler Moore Show,* Ed Asner and his pooch Gatsby faced a fork in the road when *MTM* was canceled. But his curmudgeonly creation, Lou Grant, soon got his own series in which the Minneapolis TV news producer morphed into an L.A. newspaper editor. Two decades later, Asner is still at work, recently appearing in a radio adaptation of a stage play with Carl Reiner. It was bliss, he said, "because I didn't have to get dressed up, shave or go on a diet."

ED ASNER
MARK SENNET
1978

Stray Cat

"Being in a group is not a natural thing. I find it very difficult," said Sting, frontman for one of the hottest acts of the 1980s, the Police. Touring behind *Synchronicity* was therefore both exhilarating and a chore for the singer. That hit album would be the band's last as Sting (at the keys here with Nimrod) launched out on his own, collaborating with jazzmen like Branford Marsalis. In 1992 he reunited with his former bandmates for a very exclusive show: They jammed at his wedding to Trudie Styler.

STING
IAN COOK
1983

Dogged Determination
In ratings trouble after only a few months, *Designing Women* faced cancellation. While her costars had men or children in their lives, Delta Burke, noted producer Linda Bloodworth-Thomason, "has a dog and this." Thanks in part to her own campaigning, Burke shot five more seasons until she was reportedly fired for her diva behavior. After two failed solo series, she returned to TV in 1999 as a guest on the WB series *Popular* and shared with its young stars "pearls of wisdom about what I learned in the trenches."

DELTA BURKE
MARK SENNET
1987

His Master's Voice
Manilow's chops, and his gift for penning pop hits, earned him a haul of gold records in the 1970s. "I've worked my ass off to get here," he said from the West Coast pad he shared with Bagel, his beagle, "and I'm going to work my ass off to stay here." "He's afraid it's all going to fall apart," confided a pal. Over the next two decades the former jingle writer's schmaltzy tunes did fall from favor. But in 2000, Manilow got a Grammy nod for *Manilow Sings Sinatra*—his first in 14 years.

BARRY MANILOW
STEVE SCHAPIRO
1977

Dress for Success

The more famous face is on the right. That's Battina, one of William Wegman's weimaraner supermodels. Wegman's portraits of his dogs in various stages of human dress made him a darling of the art world. When he posed with Battina at home in Maine, his New York City gallery was preparing a career retrospective. Three years later the twice-divorced artist was remarried and a father again at age 50. Renewed, he put out a picture book titled *Puppies*.

WILLIAM WEGMAN
JOHN LOENGARD
1991

Nuzzling Nobility

Though the scion of Hollywood royals Tony Curtis and Janet Leigh, Jamie Lee Curtis had to prove herself in screamer flicks like *Halloween*. By 1994 she had a plum role in *True Lies* and savored life as a wife and as a mom to two kids and retrievers Henry and Lucy. She then became the Lady Haden-Guest when her husband, director Christopher Guest, inherited an English barony. At 40, she returned to her roots with a *Halloween* sequel. "My thank-you note to the fans," said Her Ladyship.

Eyefuls "I think about these poor little creatures with no defense against their attackers. I feel sick," said France's sex kitten turned animal activist. To expose the bloody business of trapping, she cuddled a baby harp seal in Canada, then stopped when she spied its mother. "Mama Seal," said Brigitte Bardot earnestly, "I will spend my life fighting for him."

Poison Pen? Who is the viper in this picture: Truman Capote, or the stuffed version he kept on his coffee table? Author Gore Vidal, in the midst of a million-dollar libel suit, would've said the former. He charged that Capote sullied his name by telling a magazine that, 14 years earlier, Vidal had been thrown out of a White House party for drunkenness. "There's no venom like Capote's—and Gore's too—when he's on the prowl," said mutual friend George Plimpton. Refusing to settle out of court, Capote died five years later, his fortune and fangs intact.

Livin' la Vida Fido

Ricky Martin had a lot to celebrate with his golden retriever Icaro. After ending a stressful if lucrative run with the pop teen act Menudo, the Puerto Rican–born singer went solo in the Spanish-language market, and nabbed a role in a Mexican TV serial. Now he was set to crack the U.S., playing a bartender on *General Hospital*. A producer of the soap predicted, "Ricky will be very big." Bigger than she knew. In 1999 his first Anglo CD leapt off the shelf by the millions, fueled by catchy tunes and his swiveling hips. But the singer insisted that success hadn't affected him. "I don't need much," he said. "My friends, my dogs, my family, my music."

RICKY MARTIN
NEAL PRESTON
1995

My Best Friend's Vet Thing

The British government required a six-month quarantine before a dog could enter the country. This was true even if your master was possibly the year's hottest film star, the guy who stole scenes from Julia Roberts as her gay confidant in *My Best Friend's Wedding.* So London native Rupert Everett and his new black Lab Moise relocated to Paris, where they both get VIP attention at their local patisserie. Though his career took off when he started playing gay roles in Hollywood, the actor, who is himself openly gay, says, "I'm not a banner waver. I'm really a private person. I love eating in restaurants with just my dog."

RUPERT EVERETT
STEPHEN ELLISON
1997

ORIGINALS

Lest you think the world is getting too homogenous, consider these visionaries and contrarians—and their masterstrokes of inspiration

MARK SENNET/REFLEX

Beady-Eyed

Liza Lou is an artist who beards the world by beading it. Working out of Los Angeles, she bedecks everything from lawn mowers to laundry baskets with a gazillion glass beads. Despite the decorative nature of her oeuvre, cultural criticism shines through. Her take here on the *Ozzie and Harriet* era, *Kitchen*, suggests that a woman's work is never done— and took Lou five years to complete. *Backyard*, a 528-square-foot alfresco installation (replete with a bejeweled barbecue grill), speaks of her alienation from suburbia, which she refers to as a "sugarcoated dream turned toxic." Says Susan Bay of the L.A. Museum of Contemporary Art board and (with husband Leonard Nimoy) owner of a Lou: "Her work touches on the soul and how we live our lives."

LIZA LOU
MARK
SENNET
1998

Pachyderm Provocateurs

In their battle to preserve the planet, the French ecoactivists Robin des Bois (Robin Hood) deployed wit as a weapon. Here, president Jacky Bonnemains had his merry band don papier-mâché masks to trumpet their opposition to sales of ivory jewelry. "We don't want to depress people with pictures of slaughtered elephants," explained cofounder Marlène Kansas, "because depressed people don't have energy, and they need energy to help our cause."

ROBIN DES BOIS
GERARD
PLANCHENAULT
1990

Paint by Numbers

"Anyone who buys my paintings is a total fool," snorted Mark Kostabi (showing off his lucre on his New York City roof). His creations commanded thousands per canvas, though they were executed by a platoon of assistants who toiled on the time clock for as little as $4.50 per hour. Purchasers included not only Sly Stallone and David Geffen but also the Guggenheim and the Metropolitan Museum of Art. "The more I spit in their faces," he said, "the more they beg me to sell them another."

MARK KOSTABI
PETER SERLING
1988

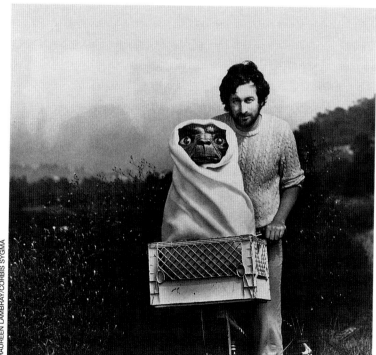

Wild Ride

Yes, he's the master of escapist blockbusters from *Jaws* to *Jurassic Park*, but Steven Spielberg proved his grown-up gravitas in the 1990s, chronicling the horrors of World War II (*Schindler's List* and *Saving Private Ryan*) and slavery (*Amistad*). And even *E.T.* had a serious meaning to its creator. Explained Spielberg, a son of divorce: "Henry's ambition to find a father by bringing E.T. into his life to fill some black hole—that was my struggle to find somebody to replace the dad who I felt had abandoned me."

STEVEN SPIELBERG
MAUREEN LAMBRAY
1982

Prince Harming

As a kid, creepy comics terrified Stephen King, but today "disease, cancer, stroke, airplane disasters" spook the master of the macabre. "It's a scary world," concedes the author of *Carrie* and *The Shining,* "and fiction is the comforting thing." Indeed, King calls chillers the "poor man's shrink"—and they may have helped him through a real-life nightmare. He was nearly killed in 1999 when a van struck him as he strolled a few miles from his summer home in North Lovell, Maine.

STEPHEN KING
JEFF JACOBSON
1980

Iconocat

"A piece of trash." That was the 1970 verdict of a Maryland judge, ruling an R. Crumb cartoon obscene. Critics were more charitable, honoring the neurotic noodler as the godfather (or at least dirty old granddad) of modern comics. Acclaimed for fathering Fritz, that X-rated cat, Crumb bounded out of the underground in 1994, starring in an eponymous documentary that won at Sundance.

R. CRUMB
ROGER RESSMEYER
1985

The King of Kink
John Waters, who created the cult classic *Pink Flamingos,* once equated someone vomiting during his movies with a standing ovation. "I've always tried to leave them gagging in the aisles," said Waters (playing a 1940s villain in his Baltimore home whose furnishings include this portrait of a murderess). Waters has since dog-paddled toward the mainstream, with hits like Johnny Depp's *Cry-Baby.* But whether his budgets are $10G or $10 mil, he prides himself on staying "a negative role model for a new generation of bored youths."

JOHN WATERS
PETER SERLING
1988

COSIMO CAVALLARO
PETER SERLING 1999

Cheeze Whiz

New York City's Washington Jefferson Hotel can blame artist Cosimo Cavallaro for its cheesy reputation. Cavallaro slathered Room 114, including even the TV and beds, with a thousand pounds of blended Swiss varieties. The Montreal-born son of a welder and a cheese merchant, he concedes that his Blue Period might cause critics to sniff: "I'm taking the risk of people saying, 'You are a fool.'"

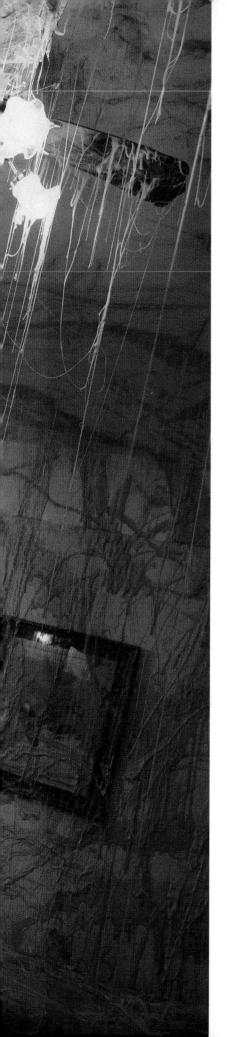

Gimme Shelter Edward and Dianna

Peden devoted 11 years to converting an abandoned nuclear missile silo near Dover, Kansas, into their subterranean four-bedroom dream house—replete with 128-square-foot skylight and a skateboard-friendly foyer. To cast away residual "negative energy," the Pedens retained a tribal medicine woman. "This place

**EDWARD &
DIANNA PEDEN**
CHIP SIMONS
1995

was built on a fear-based theory that the world needed a destructive force to remain free," explained Edward. "It's different now."

TED TURNER JAY LEVITON 1978

Boat Rocker Ever the visionary and risk-taker, Ted Turner revolutionized the media world with the first round-the-clock news channel; captured sailing's America's Cup (as skipper) and baseball's World Series (as owner of the Atlanta Braves); never failed to go for the burn, verbally (likening rival Rupert Murdoch to Hitler) or maritally (he's separated from third wife Jane Fonda); and yet still wound up with $1 billion to donate to United Nations agencies.

DIVINE
S. SILVERSTEIN 1980

Divine Mr. M

Sporting mammoth lentil-filled falsies and a blond wig, 320-pound Harris Glenn Milstead—a.k.a. Divine—didn't cut the figure of a typical film star. Of course, Divine was anything but typical, achieving infamy for vulgar on-camera stunts in John Waters' flicks. But long seeking respect as an actor, Divine finally earned a role on Fox's *Married . . . With Children* in 1988, only to suffer a fatal heart attack at 42, just hours before his first day on set.

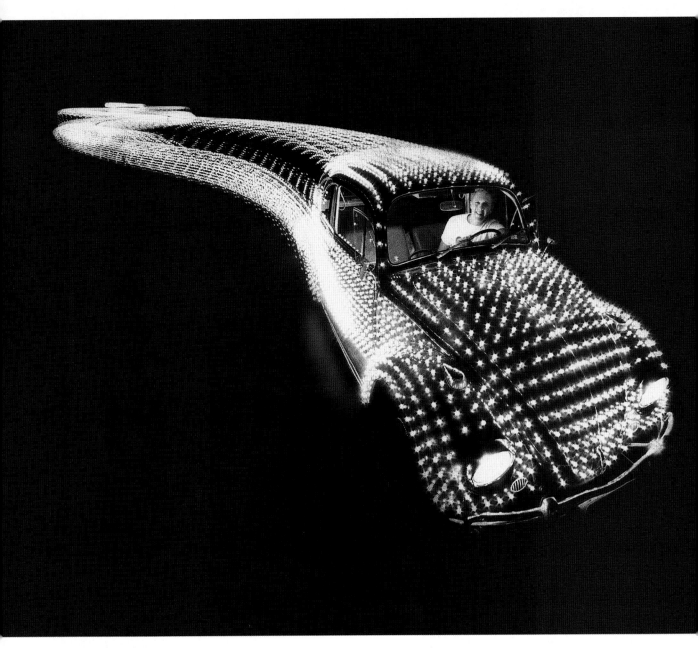

VW Bulb

The lights shone bright on Broadway, especially when Manhattan artist Eric Staller blazed by in his blinking VW Beetle. The Lightmobile, as Staller titled his customized 1967 Bug, features 1,659 bulbs flashing in 23 patterns. The car cost only $750; the generator, lights and computer to run them, $20,000. But Staller has recouped in art show appearances and a cameo delivering pizza in the 1986 film *The Money Pit*.

ERIC STALLER
ANDY LEVIN
1987

A Stitch in Twine

Francis A. Johnson made his life a ball—one of twine that wound up weighing 21,140 pounds. Housed in a shed near Darwin, Minnesota, the ball got rolling in 1950 when the hog farmer took his dad's advice never to throw anything away, collecting twine that clogged his manure spreader. A string of visitors, including CBS's Charles Kuralt, came to marvel at the monstrosity, which Johnson called "the greatest thing I ever did."

FRANCIS A. JOHNSON
TARO YAMASAKI
1986

House of Whoa!

Mark and Jackie Tresl's pet, Misha, doesn't kick up much of a fuss at meal-time. She "just eats what we eat," notes Jackie of the 1,300-pound quarter horse that sleeps on the enclosed porch of their cramped one-room log cabin in New Concord, Ohio. Initially, the Tresls allowed Misha to stay over "for just one evening" in 1986, when the then-five-month-old foal suffered from pneumonia. Within three weeks, Misha was housebroken, and Jackie later decided that "it would be inhumane to put her outside now."

CHEZ TRESL
TARO
YAMASAKI
2000

Cereal Killing

Call him a Froot Loop if you will, but Scott Bruce's collection of 5,000-plus vintage cereal boxes is now worth seven figures. "Most of this stuff ended up in landfills," says Bruce, who hunts for Cold War–era cornflakes by combing classified ads and old grocery stores. Bruce stashes his trove in secret storage sites near his home in Cambridge, Massachusetts. "I live in morbid fear of getting ripped off," admitted the Amherst College–educated former sculptor. "These boxes are going to put my kids through college."

**SCOTT
BRUCE**
BRIAN SMITH
1998

WAYNE KUSY
BLACK/TOBY 1997

Tooth Ferry

Toothpicks apparently float Wayne Kusy's boat. The Chicago marketing assistant builds models of such storied ships as the *Lusitania* using little else but toothpicks and glue. To replicate smokestacks and lifeboats, Kusy molds each mini timber with pliers until it curves. "Wayne is in the truest sense an artist," says Chicago gallery owner Celeste Sotola. "The amount of time he spends on his art is a symbol of his dedication." His *Titanic* took 18 months.

Love's Labor
Museum curators compared Joseph Furey's Brooklyn apartment to a folk art version of the Taj Mahal; honoring his late wife like the mastermind behind the Indian wonder, Furey glued and nailed every surface of his five rooms with a crazy quilt of colored tile, heart-shaped cardboard cutouts, spiral-shaped shells, painted peas, lima beans and clay birds. "I just kept decorating the place to kill time and forget some of the grief," explained the retired iron worker. Eventually he had to move in with his son, and the magical memorial soon fell victim to gentrification and floor-to-ceiling renovation.

JOSEPH FUREY
PETER SERLING
1989

MARC KLAAS
JOHN STOREY 1994

Not Forgotten

Shortly after his daughter Polly, 12, was abducted from her Petaluma, California, home and murdered, Marc Klaas gave up his rental car franchise. "I can't see myself telling people how to get to 17-Mile Drive anymore," he told his parents. "I've got to help kids." The man who killed Polly was a recent parolee, and Klaas (here with her friends) fights to keep repeat violent felons in prison. He can't save his daughter, but he can help others. "Polly," he says, "has become America's child."

An End to Silence

"The world is not ready for your family," a doctor told Elizabeth Glaser shortly after she was diagnosed as HIV-positive and had passed it to her two children. During her pregnancy with daughter Ariel in 1981, Glaser had required a transfusion and learned only years later that it was tainted. Deferring to public fear about the relatively new disease, she and her husband, actor-director Paul Michael Glaser, took just a few friends into their confidence and saw even some of them stop their kids from coming over to play. When Ariel died at seven, Elizabeth could no longer keep quiet. She started the Pediatric AIDS Foundation, and became an eloquent advocate. In six years she raised millions for research, before succumbing to the disease herself at 47. Her son Jake, 14, survives.

ELIZABETH GLASER
CHRISTOPHER LITTLE
1991

COURAGE

Rising to life's challenges and adversity, these people found themselves the heroes of very public dramas

POLLY KLAAS MEMORIAL GARDEN
FEBRUARY, 1994

IN MEMORY
POLLY HANNAH KLAAS
1981 — 1993

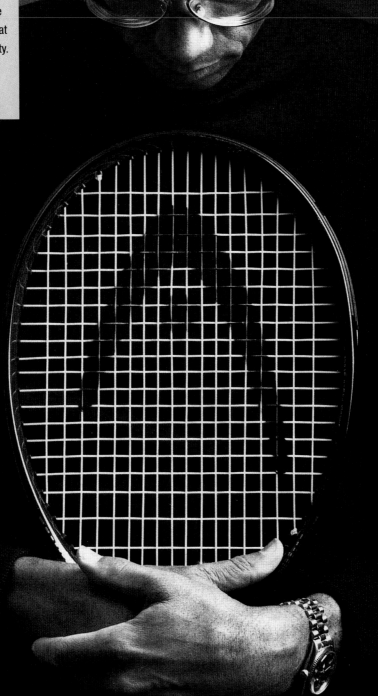

Grace Ace

Learning tennis on segregated courts in Virginia, Arthur Ashe grew up to be the first black star of the men's circuit. In retirement he was unwittingly thrust back into the spotlight when he contracted AIDS following heart surgery. Ashe had tried to keep his condition secret to protect their young daughter from what his wife Jeanne called "cruel comments that have very little to do with her reality. Her father can teach her well. He has overcome injustice before." A year later, Ashe was dead at 49.

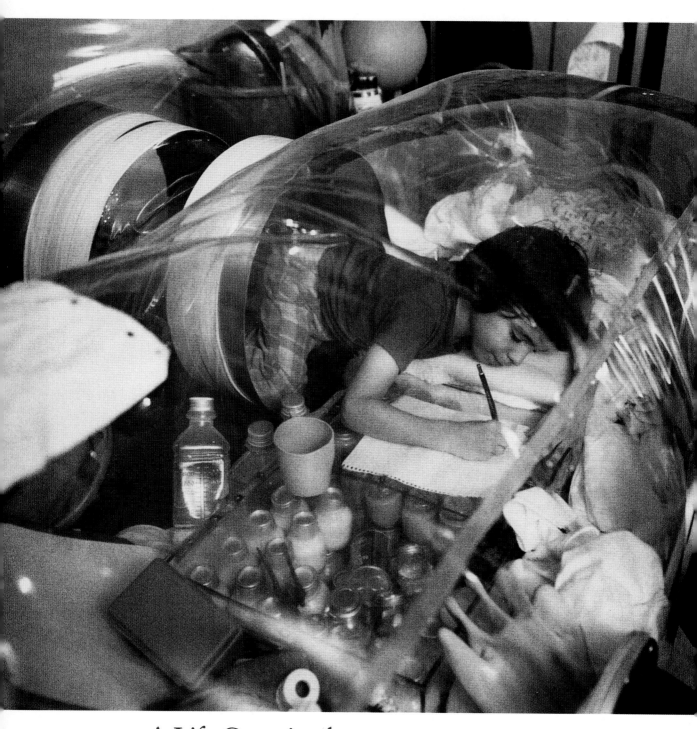

A Life Contained

David was like most kids. Some days he didn't feel like doing schoolwork, though he excelled at geography and math. He scrapped playfully with his older sister. He loved *Star Wars* movies. But David's life was far from normal. Born without an immune system, he lived in a plastic bubble to protect him from germs. Even a kiss from Mom or David Sr. (the family surname was not revealed) could kill him. New advances in bone marrow transplants seemed a cure for David when he was 12. His sister was his donor. When the procedure failed, his family knew David's struggle was ending. As a priest administered the last rites, David's mother took off her surgical gloves and touched her son's skin. "It was the first time," she said. "And the last."

DAVID
RAEANNE
RUBENSTEIN
1984

Holey Moley

In the instant that her 18-year-old mother, Cissy, stepped into her aunt's house, Jessica McClure, 18 months, slipped through the 8-inch opening of a well shaft that had been covered with a rock. Soon the Midland, Texas, backyard was filled with rescue workers, rock drillers, paramedics and pediatricians. And, of course, TV crews. Parents across the country watched in horrified anticipation. Even when it seemed her rescue was imminent, the drilling would slow because, said one volunteer, "all the men would start bawling." She emerged after 58 hours and was spirited to the hospital past cheering crowds and ringing church bells. A year later, Jessica had a thin scar on her head as evidence of the fall, but, said her father, Chip, no memory of those two terrifying days.

JESSICA McCLURE
JOE MCNALLY
1987

Hero's Welcome

A star who gained early fame in *Superman* in 1977, Christopher Reeve hadn't been seen much by the 1990s. He lived quietly with wife Dana Morosini and their son Will. After *Superman IV,* he popped up in a John Carpenter horror film, and as the lone American in a Merchant-Ivory costume drama. Then in 1995 Reeve inadvertently recaptured the world's attention. Thrown from a horse at an equestrian competition, he was instantly paralyzed. The athletic actor's body lay still and seemingly useless. "Maybe we should let me go," he told Morosini, who exhorted him, in response, "You're still you. And I love you." Soon he was acting again, and directing, as well as raising funds for spinal cord research. At the 1996 Oscars (with Susan Sarandon and his wife) he proved that he was, in fact, still himself, despite the chair and the speech halted by his ventilator. "It felt," he said, "like a homecoming."

AT THE OSCARS
ALEX BERLINER
1996

CHRISTOPHER REEVE
ROBIN BOWMAN
1994

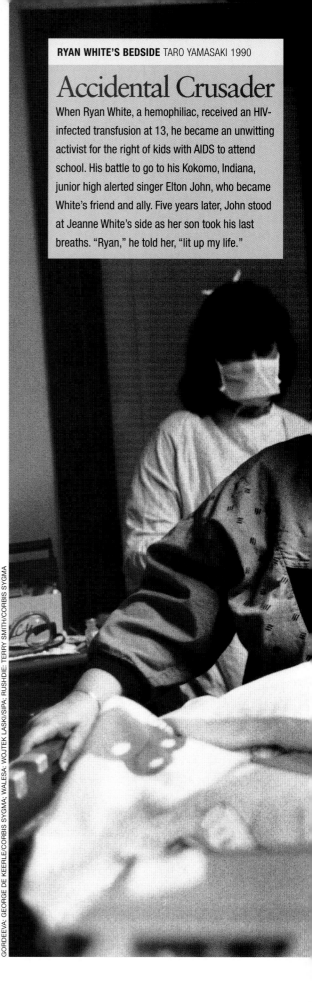

RYAN WHITE'S BEDSIDE TARO YAMASAKI 1990

Accidental Crusader

When Ryan White, a hemophiliac, received an HIV-infected transfusion at 13, he became an unwitting activist for the right of kids with AIDS to attend school. His battle to go to his Kokomo, Indiana, junior high alerted singer Elton John, who became White's friend and ally. Five years later, John stood at Jeanne White's side as her son took his last breaths. "Ryan," he told her, "lit up my life."

PRECEDING SPREAD, CLOCKWISE FROM TOP LEFT:

Alone Together
Condemned to die by Iran's Ayatollah Khomeini for perceived blasphemy in *The Satanic Verses*, Indian-born author Salman Rushdie went into hiding. So did his American wife, Marianne Wiggins, who had to cancel her own book tour. After a year in seclusion, the couple divorced. In 1999, Iran's new government

SALMAN RUSHDIE & MARIANNE WIGGINS
TERRY SMITH 1989

lifted the death warrant but couldn't end threats from Islamic extremists. Still, Rushdie went public with a new girlfriend, model Padma Lakshmi.

Stormin'
They call him the Bear: fierce as a grizzly, gentle as a teddy. The nation saw both sides of General H. Norman Schwarzkopf, who led the allied forces in the Persian Gulf War. After 239 days he marched home, victorious, to Florida and, at 56, announced his retirement. When

H. NORMAN SCHWARZKOPF
HARRY BENSON 1990

he ventured out, autograph-seekers often greeted him with stuffed bears. Marveled his sister Sally: "You would have thought he was Frank Sinatra."

Cleaning House
His son Przemak sudsed the brow that organized shipyard workers into the Solidarity trade union, thus defying and eventually toppling his Communist masters. A son of peasant farmers who became an electrician and later free Poland's

LECH WALESA
WOJTEK LASKI 1981

first president, Lech Walesa recalled, "I started out with only two things in life: a belief in God and a belief in what I was doing."

Ballet Russe
Their skating career as a pair, which began when he was 15 and she 11, led Russians Sergei Grinkov and Ekaterina Gordeeva to two Olympic golds and true love. Wed in 1991, they competed while raising daughter Daria (depicted in Red Square). But at a

EKATERINA GORDEEVA & SERGEI GRINKOV
GEORGE DE KEERLE 1995

1995 practice, Grinkov, 28, had a fatal heart attack. Four months later his young widow took the ice for the first time as a solo.

VIETNAM WAR MEMORIAL
BOB ADELMAN 1985

Forget Me Not

The Vietnam War continued to divide Americans long after the last soldiers were helicoptered from the roof of the embassy in Saigon in 1975. Seven years later, the Vietnam Veterans Memorial was unveiled in Washington, D.C., listing the 58,022 Americans who lost their lives in Southeast Asia. Mourners made rubbings of their loved ones' names. The 21-year-old Asian woman who designed this powerful tribute had given a troubled nation a healing ground.

Dumb Luck

Jim Stolpa, his wife Jennifer and their baby son Clayton drove 800 miles from California to attend a relative's funeral in Idaho, but they themselves nearly died on the way. A forecast blizzard stranded their pickup in a remote area near Vya, Nevada (population: 2), forcing the Stolpas to huddle in the cab for three chilling nights. During a break in the storm, the family trekked through the hip-high snow for help. Eventually, Jennifer and Clayton holed up in a cramped cave, while Jim, his feet frost-bitten, somehow slogged on for 48 miles. Miraculously, he was spotted by David Peterson. "[Jim] should get two medals," suggested Peterson, who also helped rescue Jennifer and Clayton. "One for stupidity and one for saving his family." But what the Stolpas couldn't save was their marriage. Their divorce, five years later, was not unfriendly; and they shared custody of their by-then two kids and lived across the street from one another.

THE STOLPA FAMILY
ACEY HARPER
1993

Degree of Difficulty

When diver Greg Louganis learned that he was HIV-positive five months before the 1988 Seoul Olympics, he responded like a champion, embarking on a grueling regimen that included AZT every four hours, a cocktail of vitamins and drugs to ward off infection, and gamma globulin infusions to bolster his immune system. "Deep down," wrote Louganis in his memoir *Breaking the Surface,* "I wanted to prove that even though I was HIV-positive, I could still win." And win he did, taking two golds despite cutting his head open during a preliminary dive. Now retired from the sport, Louganis still inspires others, volunteering for Pets Are Wonderful Support, an organization that helps AIDS patients care for their animals.

GREG LOUGANIS
CHRISTOPHER
LITTLE
1995

Gold Warrior

Her coach, Bela Karolyi, picked up a 70-pound gymnast; Kerri Strug had just lifted a nation. As the U.S. team clung to a precarious lead over Russia in the 1996 Atlanta Olympics, the 18-year-old from Tucson launched into her first vault. On the dismount, she heard her ankle snap from a serious, third-degree sprain. Strug clenched her teeth against the pain and sprinted down the runway for her required second attempt. "I knew if I didn't make it, we wouldn't win the gold," she recalled.

**KERRI STRUG &
BELA KAROLYI**
LOTA OGREN
1996

"So I said a quick prayer and asked God to help me out." After an almost perfect landing (if primarily on her right foot), she crumpled to the mat, her face twisted and in tears. Strug received a 9.712, clinching the U.S. victory.

LOTA OGREN/SIPA

HUGH HERR BARRY STAVER 1991

One Giant Step
"My doctor said I would definitely not be able to climb," recalled Hugh Herr, who at 17 lost his legs below the knees due to frostbite. On a New Hampshire outing, he and a friend had gotten trapped in the snow for two nights. But three weeks after he left rehab, he was back on the trails. "I felt wobbly, like a doe on ice," he said, "but elated." Nine years on, Herr had developed special artificial limbs for climbers and was training to run a marathon.